TIME TO QUILT

TIME TO QUILT

Fun Quilts and Retreat Ideas for 1 or 101

ANNE MOSCICKI

Martingale™
& COMPANY

That Patchwork Place® is an imprint
of Martingale & Company™.

Time to Quilt:
Fun Quilts and Retreat Ideas for 1 or 101
© 2003 by Anne Moscicki

Martingale & Company
20205 144th Avenue NE
Woodinville, WA 98072-8478 USA
www.martingale-pub.com

Printed in China
08 07 06 05 04 03   8 7 6 5 4 3 2 1

Library of Congress Cataloging-in-Publication Data
Moscicki, Anne.
   Time to quilt : fun quilts and retreat ideas for 1 or 101 / Anne Moscicki.
        p. cm.
Includes bibliographical references.
   ISBN 1-56477-473-2
   1. Patchwork—Patterns. 2. Quilting—Societies, etc.
3. Patchwork quilts. I. Title.
   TT835 .M6897 2003
   746.46—dc21
                                             2002152793

Credits

President	Nancy J. Martin
CEO	Daniel J. Martin
Publisher	Jane Hamada
Editorial Director	Mary V. Green
Managing Editor	Tina Cook
Technical Editor	Cyndi Hershey
Copy Editor	Liz McGehee
Design Director	Stan Green
Illustrator	Robin Strobel
Cover & Text Designer	Regina Girard
Photographer	Brent Kane

Mission Statement

Dedicated to providing quality products and service to inspire creativity.

Dedication

I get by with a little help from my friends.
Paul McCartney and John Lennon

And I get by very well with friends like my retreat pals: my generous sister, Julia Teters; sweet mama, Mimi Teters; brave and bouyant Karen Martinsson; patient and talented Deb Hollister; friend-for-life Linda Kenney; the irrepressible Maureen Reynolds; style-setter Cora Tunberg; Pat Zarp; Lisa White; Laura Evans; Linda Wyckoff; Kyle McAvoy; Denise Bohbot; Sybil Houghton; and Kathy Roethle. Sybil's presence at our future retreats will be a warm glow in our hearts; her inspirational dedication to living fully was cut short by cancer since our last retreat. Thank you all for sharing your time, your love, and lots of laughter and inspiration!

Acknowledgments

I am very lucky to have so many generous, enthusiastic, and encouraging friends and family members around me. As a tiny inkling grew into the book you are now holding, I have been blessed by their caring and support. The following are just a few of the many who made notable contributions.

This book would not have been possible without the unflagging help and support of my friend and partner in Touchwood Quilt Design, Linda Wyckoff. Above and beyond offering her considerable talents in the stitching, ripping, and measuring department, she contributed no small measure of patience, serenity, and gentle optimism.

My heartfelt thanks go to:

my husband, John, for providing me with encouragement, time, and space to surround myself with quilts;

my beautiful daughters, Christine and Catherine, who provide me with both comic relief and the multiple interruptions that I have come to recognize as the balance I need in my life;

Jennifer Lokey, Linda Kenney, and Maureen Reynolds, who cheered me on from the start;

Mary Green, Karen Soltys, and Cyndi Hershey, who listened patiently and advised as my ideas grew into reality; and the enthusiastic creative staff at Martingale including Stan Green and Brent Kane;

Celeste Marshall, whose talents added the finishing touch on many projects throughout this book;

and so many other friends and acquaintances whose inquiries, comments, and encouragement buoyed me on a daily basis.

CONTENTS

WISH YOU WERE HERE

I have looked forward to this particular Saturday morning for months. My second cup of coffee steams in my hands, and my sewing machine vies for my attention, as does the aroma of the muffins baking in the kitchen. A fire crackles in the fireplace, and the room hums with the happy conversation of ten of my dearest quilting friends.

At this moment, I am content as a warm cat, and Sunday afternoon and the drive home to my real life—work, telephone messages, the dishwasher, my daughters' math homework and music practice—seem a million miles away, and for now, I'll just leave them there. We are all spending the weekend in a lovely home on the scenic Oregon coast, at the retreat we look forward to each year. We offer each other quilting advice, teach each other our quilting tricks, and share our fabrics and our lives for this one weekend each year.

As pleased as I am by the progress made on whatever quilt I take to this annual retreat, this shared time has added a true and satisfying richness to my life. Far from the ugly, gossipy misnomer "stitch-'n'-bitch," our conversations have been a window to the hearts of women possessed of determination, vitality, and joy.

They have struggled with cancer and "the terrible twos," buried children and raised teenagers, lost love and found it again, loved laughter and maintained hope. They are a source of strength and inspiration that I could not have tapped into without setting aside this one weekend each year.

We mark our calendars months in advance, not just setting the days aside, but protecting them from the demands of work and family. We have found ways to skimp on the dollar expenses as we splurge on the elemental luxury of friendship. We set the time aside to quilt, and we all sew up a storm, both on our own projects and our annual charity quilt. But quilting is only the colorful backdrop to the friendships formed. This is not idle time. These are life lessons shared . . . and a quilt to show for it!

So, I'll be staying in my jammies and slippers for awhile, just because I can! After lunch, I'll join Cora and Karen for a walk on the beach, while my sister Julia and a few others head into town to visit a quilt shop. Then I'll sew until dinner, when we'll vote on our charity quilt this year, and then—maybe—stay up with Pat and Julia to quilt and chat through the wee hours. Wish you were here. . . .

Anne

BEYOND THE QUILTING BEE

More than a century ago, quilting bees filled the same dual purpose that a modern quilting retreat does: to create beautiful, functional quilts, and answer a genuine need for friendship and community. Colonial and pioneer women gathered to stitch at a time when lonely physical distances separated them, occasionally bridged by letters or a traveler's secondhand news.

Typically, women pieced their quilt tops during the cold winter—quilting on a traditional, large frame was impractical in small homes heated only with a fireplace. But during the warmer months, as travel became easier, friends, neighbors, and family gathered to share the work, the joys of accomplishment, and a sense of belonging. Quilting, barn raising, sheep shearing, harvest, building a school, and other labors became community events inspiring friendship, food, and festivities.

After a long, lonely winter, what a joy it must have been for a pioneer wife to plan an event like a quilting bee! The simple pleasures of time spent with other women! Preparations were made ahead of time—food planned, house cleaned—and anticipation made the extra work seem easy. Then friends arrived and needles flew, the cooking fire crackled, and conversations and friendships blossomed as the events of the winter were discussed and news passed along. Practical matters were surely not overlooked: these women shared their successes and concerns with every subject from chickens to childbirth, and were surely the richer for it, both practically and emotionally.

Today, most of the women I know use email and answering machines to bridge a gap created by Little League schedules, commutes, and the complexities of dual-income families. But these technologies can only exchange information and will never replace the heartfelt conversation that grows out of the small luxury of shared time.

The time our group spends together each year as we cut, iron, quilt, talk, sew, and cook is the time needed to get to know each other that well. Help someone trim her nine hundred 1½" triangle points for her daughter's king-sized Feathered Star wedding quilt, and you'll learn something significant about each other!

These quilting retreats provide a balance in our lives. We face the impersonal nature of business, technology, and the whirlwind of day-to-day life in the new century. Quilting provides us with a relaxed sense of sharing in both a historical continuum and a circle of friends. In quilting retreats today, as in quilting bees of the past, the outcome is shared fabrics and lifelong friendships.

A QUILTING STATE OF MIND

Whether you have a weekend or an afternoon, a retreat is purely a state of mind. Of course, it's easier to leave the laundry and dishwasher and errands behind when you turn your quilting retreat into a mini-vacation, as my friends and I do once a year. But you can also declare yourself "in retreat" for an afternoon with a little advance planning.

Throughout this book, you'll find suggestions for making the time you sew a rejuvenation of your creativity, spirit, and friendships. You'll find projects to suit your timetable and your personal style, whether you have a weekend or an afternoon, with friends or without. My sincerest hope is that you'll find the inspiration to give the gift of time to yourself.

EASIER THAN YOU THINK

Though many retreats are offered by renowned instructors and quilt artists or through quilt shops or guilds, we all come with our own agenda: primarily to quilt, but also to rejuvenate at our individual paces. This book will show you how easy it is to organize the retreat you and your quilting friends want, and for a price that you are comfortable paying.

MY HEART'S CONTENT

You've set aside some time and now you can quilt to your heart's content! Chain piecing and fusible appliqué make this lovely little quilt a snap to stitch in a weekend. As a retreat project, it's a natural for fabric and block swaps in any fabric combination your retreat group desires. Personalize the bonus project, Anytime Valentine Hearts, on page 19, with embroidered messages and fill the hearts with stuffing, rice, beans, or scents.

MY HEART'S CONTENT QUILT

BLOCK SIZE: 12"

MATERIALS

Yardage is based on 42"-wide fabric unless otherwise indicated.

1 yd. of white for background

½ yd. *each* of light blue and dark blue prints for Diamond blocks and cornerstones

2¼ yds. of medium blue print for hearts, inner border, outer border, and binding

¼ yd. *each* of 12 assorted light to medium blue prints for piano-key units and pieced border

3¼ yds. for backing

Twin-size batting (62" x 74")

¾ yd. paper-backed fusible web

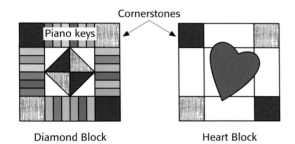

Diamond Block   Heart Block

CUTTING

From each of the 12 assorted ¼-yd. light to medium blue prints, cut:
- 3 strips, 1½" x 42"; crosscut each strip in half, 1½" x 21"

From each of the two ½-yd. light blue and dark blue prints, cut:
- 1 strip, 3⅞" x 42"; crosscut into 6 squares, 3⅞" x 3⅞"
- 3 strips, 3½" x 42"; crosscut into 24 squares, 3½" x 3½"

From the white fabric, cut:
- 1 strip, 6½" x 42"; crosscut into 6 squares, 6½" x 6½"
- 2 strips, 3⅞" x 42"; crosscut into 12 squares, 3⅞" x 3⅞"
- 4 strips, 3½" x 42"; crosscut into 24 rectangles, 3½" x 6½"

From the medium blue print, cut:
- 5 strips, 1½" x 42"
- 6 strips, 6½" x 42"
- 7 strips, 2½" x 42"

ASSEMBLING THE BLOCKS AND BORDER

1. Sew the 1½" x 21" strips together into 9 strip sets of 6 strips each. Press the seams open. These sets will measure 6½" x 21". Cut each strip set into three 3½" x 6½" piano-key units for a total of 24 units. Reserve the remaining strip sets for the pieced border.

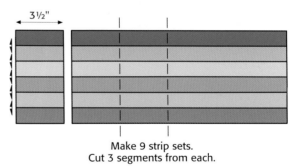

Make 9 strip sets.
Cut 3 segments from each.

2. Choose 12 of these 3½" x 6½" piano-key units and add a light blue 3½" square to one end. Press toward the piano-key units. Add a dark blue 3½" square to the opposite end. You will now have 12 piano-key-and-cornerstone units, and 12 piano-key units.

Add cornerstones to ends.

MY HEART'S CONTENT QUILT

Designed by Anne Moscicki, Lake Oswego, Oregon, 2001, 52" x 64".
Pieced by Anne Moscicki and Linda Wyckoff; quilted by Celeste Marshall.

3. With right sides together, layer one 3⅞" white square with one 3⅞" light blue square. Draw a line diagonally from corner to corner on the white square. Sew ¼" from the line on both sides, then cut the square in half on the line. Open each half-square-triangle unit and press the seam toward the background fabric. Repeat, using the remaining 3⅞" white and 3⅞" dark blue squares.

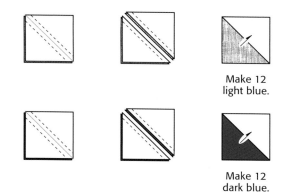

Make 12 light blue.

Make 12 dark blue.

4. Arrange 2 *each* of the light blue and dark blue half-square-triangle units into a block. The light blue triangles should point toward each other, and the dark blue triangles as well. Join the units into 2 pairs, pressing the seams in alternate directions. Join the pairs and press.

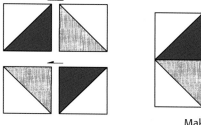
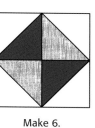

Make 6.

5. Add one piano-key unit to each side of the Diamond blocks and press toward the piano-key units. Add one piano-key-and-cornerstone unit to the top and bottom to complete each Diamond block. Be sure to pay attention to the placement of the light and dark cornerstones. Press. Make 6 Diamond blocks.

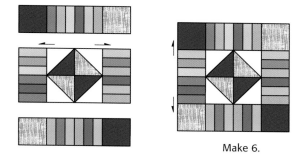

Make 6.

6. Sew a 3½" x 6½" white rectangle to opposite sides of a 6½" white square. Press toward the square. Make 6 units. Sew a light blue 3½" cornerstone to one end of the remaining twelve 3½" x 6½" background rectangles. Repeat, using the dark blue 3½" squares for the opposite end. Press toward the squares. Make 12 of these units. Join one of these units to the top and bottom of each background rectangle-square unit. Pay attention to the placement of the light and dark cornerstones. Press.

7. Using the template on page 21, trace 6 hearts onto the paper side of the fusible web. Cut slightly beyond the traced line of each heart. Press each heart, paper side up, onto the wrong side of the medium blue print according to the fusible web instructions. Cut out the 6 hearts. Peel off the paper backing and arrange the hearts at playful angles on each Heart block. Press. Use a buttonhole stitch around each heart to secure it to the quilt or try using one of your machine's decorative stitches. Refer to "Tips for Decorative Stitching" on page 41.

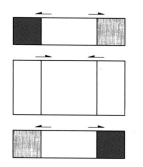
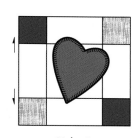

Make 6.

8. Stitch the reserved piano-key strip sets into 2 groups of 3 sets each, measuring approximately 10½" x 18½". From each strip set cut 6 pieces, 1½" x 18½". Join 3 pieces for one side of the pieced border. Press the seams open. Repeat with the remaining pieces to make a total of 4 pieced border units.

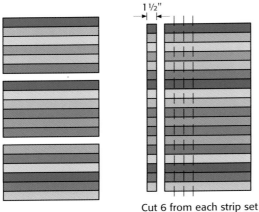

Cut 6 from each strip set
(12 total).

9. Lay out the blocks and sew them into rows. Press. Join the rows. Press.

10. Add the 3 borders, referring to "Adding Borders" on page 91. Begin with the 1½" medium blue inner border, then the pieced piano-key border, and finally the 6½" medium blue outer border. After measuring, you will need to remove the extra portion of the piano-key border so that it is the correct length for your quilt.

FINISHING THE QUILT

1. Refer to "Quilting Basics" on page 89 as needed to finish your quilt. Prepare the quilt backing, then layer and baste the backing, batting, and quilt top together.

2. Quilt as desired. In the quilt pictured, a small medallion design was quilted on point in each Diamond block. The hearts were stippled and then echo-quilted.

3. Trim the excess batting and backing fabric, remove the basting, and bind your quilt. Use the seven 2½"-wide medium blue strips for the binding.

4. Add a hanging sleeve if desired. Add a label or pocket to your quilt.

My Heart's Content Quilt

Reproduction fabrics add vintage charm to the playful appliquéd heart motif.

Designed by Anne Moscicki, Lake Oswego, Oregon, 2001, 52" x 64".
Pieced by Linda Wyckoff; quilted by Celeste Marshall.

Making Your Home a Quilting Haven

Wouldn't you love to spend the whole afternoon quilting, with no distractions? It's not impossible! Try some of the strategies here to declare the space and time for yourself.

- Write it on the calendar: "noon–6 PM: Mom at Quilting Retreat." This is not just an indulgence; it's a healthy antidote to daily life that just happens to feel like an indulgence.

- Say no, politely but firmly, to all other opportunities to be distracted from your project: "Thank you for the invitation, but I have already made plans for Saturday afternoon." "I'd love to help out with the concession stand (potluck, fund-raiser) another time, but I already have plans for that afternoon." After all, you have made other plans, whether you're at home, two hundred miles away at a mountain cabin, or at a doctor's appointment.

- Don't pretend that you can take "just a few minutes" to run to the grocery store; the momentum you lose on your project will cost you much more than that, and the magical spell of the retreat will be broken.

- Make generous use of tact; after all, you want the rest of the family out of the house for the day, and with smiles on their faces when you see them again!

- Talk to your family beforehand about your retreat plan and your expectations. You don't have to be off-limits to them, but (depending on age and abilities) tell them you expect them to be responsible for their own meals and transportation. Their respect of your time and space will surely be reciprocated in the two-way street of family life.

- This is not a bad time for gentle reminders that your husband's football games are also showing at his buddy's house or on the big screen at the sports bar downtown.

- If you must resort to drastic measures, declare "Deep Cleaning Day": everyone left in the house will be issued rubber gloves and toothbrushes and expected to participate fully. Just watch them disappear!

- Barter child-care favors. Remember when you took your neighbor's kids to a movie and the pool on the day she needed help? It's your turn to cash in. If you haven't taken the neighbor's kids to a movie and the pool for awhile, schedule it when you ask her to take your kids for a day.

- Plan ahead for family meals. This is the day for a slow-simmer recipe that goes into the pot first thing in the morning, leaving you free to stir up some more important things from your stash. Or pull out a casserole from the freezer. Even easier: pizza delivery!

- Now that everyone else is taken care of, don't forget to plan ahead for yourself! What is going to make this afternoon feel like a minivacation? It could be as simple as a vase of flowers in the windowsill and your favorite CDs at hand, as luxurious as ordering Chinese food to be delivered for lunch, or as indulgent as having your favorite cookie dough ready in the fridge for a snack. Lay out your fabrics and tools in place the night before so that you can just walk in and begin quilting.

ANYTIME
VALENTINE HEARTS

Why wait until Valentine's Day? Stitch up these sweet little hugs and kisses for everybody whenever Cupid strikes! Be creative: add buttons, ribbons, bows, or tassels; use pinking shears to cut them out and leave the edges rough; make a ruffle for the edges; add a ribbon hanger; adorn them with your sweetie's initials or a favorite appliqué; write a love note, wish, or poem in permanent pen . . . there's no end to the possibilities!

MATERIALS

For each heart, you will need:

1 fat quarter or 2 squares of fabric at least 8" x 8"

Approximately 1 to 2 cups of rice, beans, or potpourri for filling, or use polyester fiberfil

Ribbon or bead trim, embroidery floss, or other embellishments (optional)

ASSEMBLING THE HEARTS

1. Photocopy or trace the heart pattern on page 21 onto a separate sheet of paper and cut it out on the solid outer line. Fold the fat quarter in half or layer the 8" squares. Pin the pattern to the fabric. Cut around the edge of the pattern. Add any *fusible* embellishments at this point if desired.

2. With right sides together, pin the layers together along the edges. Add a ruffle at this point if desired; refer to instructions at right. Stitch with a ¼" seam allowance, leaving the indicated area open for filling or stuffing. Clip the curves and trim the point at the bottom of the heart. Turn the heart right side out. Fill or stuff the heart and stitch to close the opening.

3. Add ribbons, tassels, buttons, or a hanger as desired.

Pretty in Pinked

The easiest way to make these little loves is to cut out the heart shape with pinking shears. With wrong sides together, stitch ¼" from the edge, leaving an opening for stuffing. After inserting your choice of filling, place the heart back in your sewing machine and stitch the opening closed. For variety, try using different thread colors and one of your machine's decorative stitches.

Adding a Ruffle

A piece of leftover binding would work beautifully for the ruffle; just add a hem fold at each end.

1. Cut a 2½" x 34" strip. Fold each end under ¼" and press. Fold the strip in half lengthwise and press again.

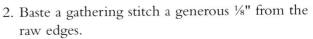

2. Baste a gathering stitch a generous ⅛" from the raw edges.
3. Gather the strip to a length of 22½".

4. With one of the hearts right side up, pin the gathered edge of the ruffle to the raw edge of the heart, with the gathers facing the right side. Begin and end the ruffle at the indentation at the top of the heart, overlapping the hemmed ends by ¼". You'll have some bulk at the lower point of the heart; pin carefully to avoid catching the folded edge of the ruffle in the seam. Baste, if desired. Place the remaining heart on top, with right sides together, and pin. Stitch ¼" from the raw edges, concealing the gathering stitch in the seam allowance. Clip into the V of the heart, being careful not to cut into the seam. Slightly trim the point of the heart, if desired, to reduce bulk.

Leave open.

5. Turn the heart right side out and fill with rice, beans, potpourri, or polyester fiberfill. From the back of the heart, blindstitch the opening closed.

Adding Initials

Where to find a lovely letter? Try looking through magazines or books for larger-than-text letters, or ask for typography books at the library and photocopy to size. You may have beautiful typefaces on your home computer, too! Go through the fonts in your word processing program and size them appropriately.

If you're using fusible appliqué, try to find a typeface that has wide strokes in the letters. A delicate initial with scrolls and swirls may be better suited to embroidery or permanent fabric pens.

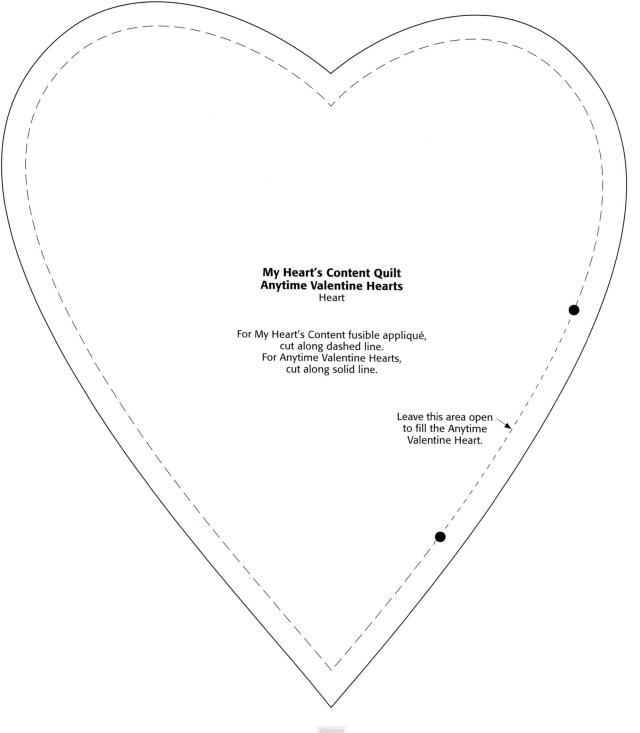

My Heart's Content Quilt
Anytime Valentine Hearts
Heart

For My Heart's Content fusible appliqué,
cut along dashed line.
For Anytime Valentine Hearts,
cut along solid line.

Leave this area open
to fill the Anytime
Valentine Heart.

REUNION STAR

Simplicity makes this quilt an excellent choice for a block trade, a special community quilt, or a group gift to a friend in need of a warm hug. Nine Patch blocks are so simple that even a novice can contribute to this quilt, and the starry sashing adds sparkle. Enjoy the easy flip-and-sew techniques and embellish with machine decorative stitching if you want.

REUNION STAR QUILT

BLOCK SIZE: 12"

MATERIALS

Yardage is based on 42"-wide fabric unless otherwise indicated.

24 assorted fat quarters, coordinated into pairs for Nine Patch blocks, or a variety of assorted prints that measure at least 4½" x 4½"

1 yd. of burgundy print for sashing

½ yd. of light fabric for cornerstone stars

2¾ yds. of rose print for borders and binding

4 yds. for backing

Twin-size batting (70" x 84")

CUTTING

From each coordinated pair of fat quarters, cut:
- 4 squares, 4½" x 4½", from 1 print, and 5 squares, 4½" x 4½", from its coordinate. You will have enough leftover fabric to repeat each print in another block if desired.

From the burgundy print, cut:
- 11 strips, 2½" x 42"; crosscut into 31 rectangles, 2½" x 12½"

From the light fabric, cut:
- 5 strips, 2½" x 42"; crosscut into 80 squares, 2½" x 2½"

From the rose print, cut:
- 7 strips, 6½" x 42"
- 7 strips, 2½" x 42"; crosscut into 14 rectangles, 2½" x 14½"; 2 rectangles, 2½" x 4½", and 24 squares, 2½" x 2½"
- 8 strips, 2½" x 42"

ASSEMBLING THE BLOCKS

1. Arrange the coordinating squares in a pleasing layout. Sew the squares into 3 rows of 3 squares each. Press the seam allowances in alternate directions in each row. Join the rows, butting the opposing seam allowances and pinning to match the seams.

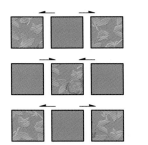 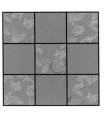

Make 12.

REUNION STAR QUILT

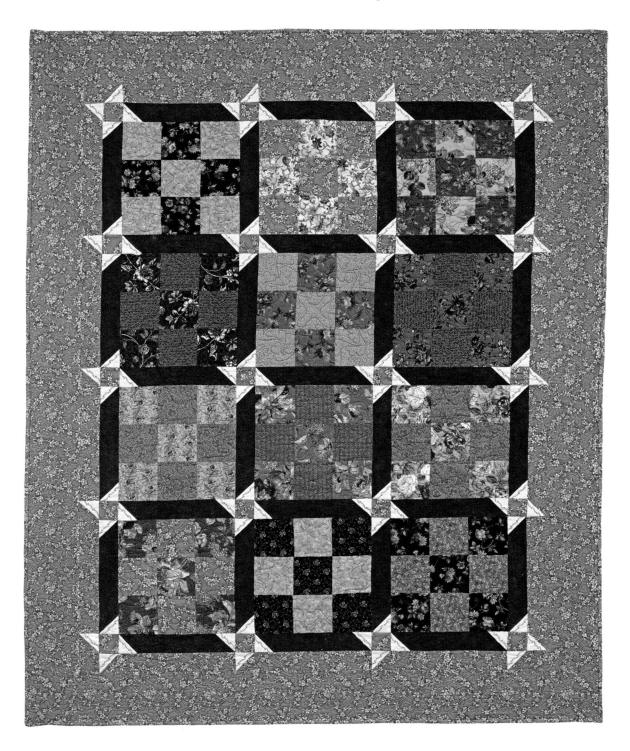

Designed by Anne Moscicki, Lake Oswego, Oregon, 2001, 60" x 74".
Pieced by Anne Moscicki and Linda Wyckoff; quilted by Celeste Marshall.

◇ NOTE ◇
Follow the sashing cornerstone illustrations carefully to make sure your sashing strips form twinkling cornerstone stars.

2. With right sides together, layer one 2½" light square over the end of one 2½" x 12½" burgundy rectangle. Draw a line diagonally from corner to corner on the square and sew on the line. Cut ¼" from the line. Open the light triangle to create the star tip. Press toward the rectangle.

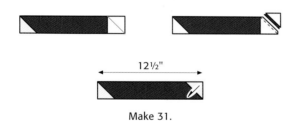

3. Repeat at the opposite end of the burgundy rectangle. Be sure that the seams are sewn in the correct direction. If desired, add a decorative stitch to embellish the star tips as shown in the quilt on the facing page. Refer to "Tips for Decorative Stitching" on page 41.

12½"

Make 31.

4. Lay out the Nine Patch blocks, sashing, and 2½" rose squares. Distribute the colors and ensure the correct placement of sashing stars. Sew 5 horizontal sashing rows, each consisting of 3 sashing units and 4 cornerstone squares. Press toward the squares. Sew 1 sashing unit

vertically at the beginning and end of the block rows as well as between the blocks. Press toward the blocks. Sew the sashing rows to the block rows. Press toward the blocks.

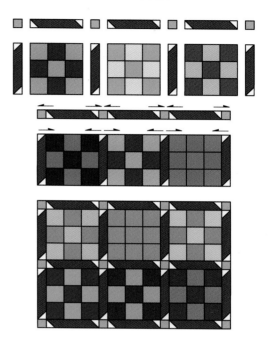

5. With right sides together, layer one 2½" light square over the end of one 2½" x 14½" rose rectangle. Draw a line diagonally from corner to corner on the square and sew on the line. Cut ¼" from the line. Open the triangle to create the star tip. Press toward the rectangle. If desired, add a decorative stitch to embellish the star tip. Refer to "Tips for Decorative Stitching" on page 41. Repeat to make 14 star-point border units, 2½" x 14½"; 2 border units, 2½" x 4½"; and 2 border squares, 2½" x 2½".

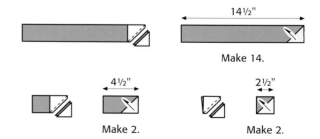

14½"

Make 14.

4½"

Make 2.

2½"

Make 2.

ASSEMBLING THE BORDERS

1. Join the star-point border sections to create the 4 star-point borders. As you join them, note the orientation of each piece.

   Border A: from left to right, one 2½" x 2½" unit and three 2½" x 14½" units

   Border B: from left to right, three 2½" x 14½" units and one 2½" x 2½" unit

   Border C: from top to bottom, one 2½" border-fabric square, four 2½" x 14½" units, and one 2½" x 4½" unit

   Border D: from top to bottom, one 2½" x 4½" unit, four 2½" x 14½" units, and one 2½" border-fabric square

   Join the borders to the pieced center of the quilt, beginning with A and B. Use pins to match the seams, referring to "Easing in Techniques" on page 90. Repeat with C and D. Press toward the borders.

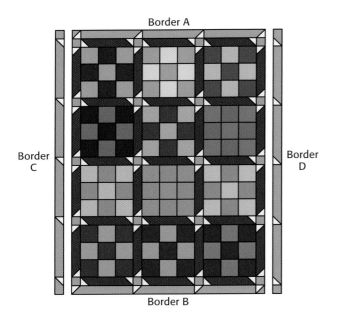

Border A

Border C

Border D

Border B

2. Join two 6½"-wide outer border strips for each of the two sides of the quilt. Cut one of the remaining strips in half to 6½" x 21". Join one 21" strip to the end of each remaining full outer border strip to be used for the top and bottom of the quilt. Measure and sew the outer borders to the quilt, following the instructions for "Adding Borders" on page 91.

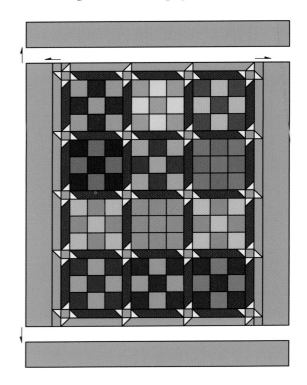

FINISHING THE QUILT

1. Refer to "Quilting Basics" on page 89 as needed to finish your quilt. Prepare the quilt backing; then layer and baste the backing, batting, and quilt top together.

2. Quilt as desired.

3. Trim the excess batting and backing fabric, remove the basting, and bind your quilt. Use the eight 2½"-wide rose strips for the binding.

4. Add a hanging sleeve if desired. Add a label or pocket to your quilt.

Siesta Simmer

Since our annual retreat usually falls on Cinco de Mayo weekend, we feel compelled to make a fiesta out of it! Tangy lemonade, sangria, or margaritas set the mood for a relaxing dinner and drawn-out conversation.

Put this ultimate no-fuss, low-fat meal on to cook in the morning, let it simmer until it's done, then reheat for dinnertime. Use your crock pot according to the manufacturer's instructions if you prefer it to the stovetop. The chicken can be made two weeks ahead and frozen.

Serve with rice or tortillas, or on chips for nachos. Add your favorite south-of-the-border accompaniments to the buffet: chopped lettuce and onion; diced tomatoes; olives; corn; chopped cilantro; nonfat sour cream; guacamole; grated jack, cheddar, or Colby cheese; and more salsa. With the exception of lettuce and tomatoes, the accompaniments can be prepared a day in advance and stored in plastic bags or ready-to-serve plastic storage containers to travel to the retreat.

Pollo con Salsa

3 pounds frozen, boneless, skinless chicken breasts

1 jar (14 ounces) of your favorite salsa

1 cup water

Place all ingredients in a large saucepan; you need not defrost the chicken. Place over medium heat, allowing the mixture to come to a simmer. Cover and adjust heat to maintain a slow simmer for 5 or more hours, stirring occasionally, until chicken shreds easily. Add more water during cooking, if necessary, to keep chicken from becoming dry; if desired, uncover and continue simmering until sauce is thick.

Serves 12, generously.

Cowboy Beans

1 pound dried pinto beans, picked over and rinsed

2 cans (6 ounces) diced mild green chilies

2 chicken bouillon cubes (6 grams)

1 medium onion, chopped (optional)

1 tablespoon garlic, minced (optional)

2 to 3 teaspoons cumin (optional)

Salt

Place all ingredients except salt in a large pot and cover with water. Cover and simmer several hours, stirring occasionally, until beans are tender. Using the back of a wooden spoon, mash some of the beans against the side of the pot. Salt to taste.

Serves 10 to 12.

TOASTY TOES FOOT WARMER

Each square in this Nine Patch block is really a little pillow pocket filled with aromatic rice. Heat the finished project in the microwave for a minute or two and warm your tootsies!

MATERIALS

Yardage is based on 42"-wide fabric unless otherwise indicated.

9 assorted 4½" flannel squares for Puff blocks

9 assorted 4" cotton squares for lining

15" square for backing

¼ yd. for binding

15" square of polyester batting

Approximately 3 cups aromatic rice, such as jasmine

#8 perle cotton for tassels

ASSEMBLING THE PUFF BLOCKS

Relax and enjoy these funny little pillow blocks! It doesn't matter which direction your tucks go or whether they are in the exact center. Note that you will use a ⅛" seam allowance while making each individual block.

1. With wrong sides together, layer one 4½" flannel square over one 4" lining square, matching the top and left sides.

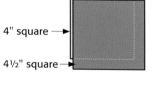

4" square →
4½" square →

2. Pinch a small tuck in the left side of the flannel square, taking up just enough fabric to align the bottom edges of the flannel and lining.

⅛"

3. Pin the tuck into place and stitch, using a ⅛" seam allowance.

4. Repeat the tucking and pinning on 2 more sides. You will have created a little "pot-bellied pocket."

Make 9.

STUFFING THE PUFFS

1. Stuff each pocket with about ⅓ cup of the rice. A small funnel is helpful but not required. You may want to work on a jelly roll pan or a tray with sides to keep any errant rice grains from falling on the floor.

2. After the rice is in the pocket, repeat the tucking and pinning on the last side.

3. Stitch the pocket closed with a ⅛" seam allowance.

4. As you sew, avoid running over the rice grains with your sewing machine. Push all the rice grains away from the seam line and use one or two pins to hold the rice in place.

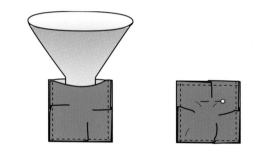

JOINING THE PUFFS

As you stitch, remember that the texture of the pocket blocks will minimize most any mistakes in seam allowance. Attach your walking foot to your sewing machine if you have one. It will make joining the pocket blocks easier. Bonus: no pressing seam allowances! Once again, pin as necessary to avoid sewing over the grains of rice.

1. Lay out the pocket blocks in a Nine Patch design.

2. With tucked sides facing together, stitch the puffs together into rows, using a ¼" seam allowance. This ¼" seam allowance will cover the previous ⅛" seam allowance.

3. Join the rows. Place a pin at each matching seam allowance as well as in the middle of each puff. Don't fret about seam allowances not matching perfectly! You are working with a lot of fabric and bulky filling to create a very textural little quilt. If you're not certain, turn the first row over and take a look; see how the seams hide in the "valleys" between the blocks.

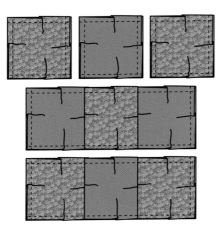

FINISHING THE FOOT WARMER

1. Lay the filled Nine Patch on your work surface, right side up. If you are adding tassels to the corners, pin them into place, facing to the center of the Nine Patch.

2. Layer the backing square, wrong side down, on top of the batting square. With right sides together, center the Nine Patch on the backing square. The backing will be layered between the Nine Patch and batting.

3. Pin all the seams and corners. Using a walking foot, stitch around the Nine Patch, leaving a 5½" open space along one edge. As you stitch, avoid running over any rice grains. You may want to add additional pins to keep the rice grains toward the center of the Nine Patch. Trim the batting and backing even with the Nine Patch. Clip the corners at an angle to help reduce bulk.

4. Turn the foot warmer right side out and whip-stitch the opening closed.

5. Tie the layers at the 4 interior corners of the center puff, using perle cotton. Pass the needle up through the foot warmer backing very close to one of the interior corner seams. Return it back through the layered foot warmer to the back, taking a small stitch. Remove the needle and tie a square knot to secure the layers. Trim the ends of the perle cotton about 1" from the knot. Repeat with the remaining 3 interior corner seams.

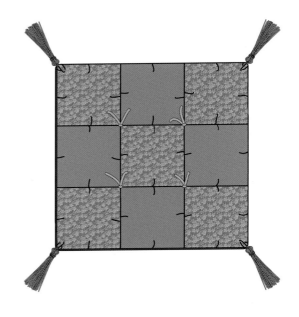

Heat your foot warmer in the microwave for a minute or two. Check on it often (once a minute or so) to avoid a dangerously high temperature. When checking the temperature, pick up the foot warmer and redistribute the rice grains within the pockets, because microwaves heat unevenly. Now enjoy the sensation of toasty toes!

Creating a Group Quilt

Sending the work of your hands out into your community can only come back to you in good ways. Whether you and your friends send the fruits of your labor into the arms of a hurt or lonely individual, a mentoring program, a halfway house, or any other worthwhile venue, you will feel the joy of belonging to a solution. Many hands do make light work! At the same time, you are giving yourself a gift of shared time with friends as well as time to quilt.

PUTTING THE QUILT TO ITS BEST USE

When we think of creating a group quilt, we often think of finding someone who will actually use it for comfort and warmth. Typical recipients might be a program that is helping women to escape domestic violence or an agency that helps children who have been abused. Sometimes it's more personal, such as a friend in need of support or an individual who deserves special acknowledgment. These are excellent ways to put a community quilt to good use by providing real comfort to the user.

Also, consider using the quilt to generate money for a worthy cause. Finding an organization that will raffle or auction the quilt can generate goodwill within your community that extends far beyond one individual.

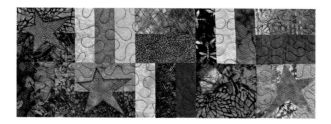

COORDINATING A SUCCESSFUL GROUP QUILT

Planning a group quilt is a little like hosting a potluck dinner: you don't know if you'll have three potato salads or a dozen desserts! It's just left to chance, but everyone leaves with a satisfied appetite and the joy of the experience. Unlike a potluck, a quilt lasts a long time. Keeping a few guidelines in mind will help to make the quilt one of which everyone can be proud.

Design
If the quilt is for one particular person, find out the recipient's favorite colors or home-decor preferences and use those as a guide.

If this quilt is destined for a specific cause, find out if a theme for pattern, print, or color may be appropriate. For example, a quilt that will be auctioned to provide funds for a community garden would be perfect in floral, fruit, and vegetable prints. A quilt going to a children's hospital could be made using pastels in the classic Tumbling Blocks pattern. A quilt that goes to comfort a victim of abuse might be made of warm, snuggly flannel. Use your imagination!

Pattern
Match the skill level of the participants to the complexity of the pattern. Neighbor's Fence (page 44) is a wonderful pattern for a group quilt because even a true beginner can create the blocks with just a bit of rotary-cutting advice. Blocks that require matching seams, templates, or triangles require a bit more skill from the participants. Send a photo or diagram of the pattern to everyone so that they can envision the final result.

Color

Avoid direct color names unless you're asking for the full range of color. Your idea of "the perfect orange" may clash horribly with someone else's, but making a quilt from "every shade of orange possible" could be intriguing!

As you specify fabrics, use broadly descriptive words that evoke colors, moods, themes, and fabric groups. Remember to specify flannels or cottons. Here are some examples:

- Sun-drenched, island-happy batiks

- Autumn-hued flannels in rustic plaids and prints

- Sweet reproductions in fresh ice-cream colors

- Romantic garden prints in soft pastels

- Vivid electric shades and funky bold prints

- Fresh primary prints and colors from the crayon box

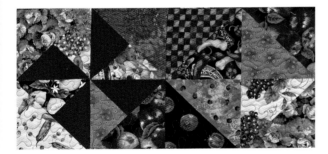

It's best to keep your directions in a positive tone. However, for clarity, specify what you don't want. For example:

- No gold print on the fabrics, please!

- Grab the creamy, off-white shades from your stash for this project, as we are striving for a "country" look. No bright white, please!

- This quilt should look fresh and crisp, so please choose fabric with clean, bright whites!

OOOOPS!

What if the blocks really don't look good together? Split the blocks into groups that do coordinate well and make two or more smaller quilts or projects.

Finally, let go and enjoy the process. Odds are that this quilt won't look at all like the one you had pictured. However, the energy and variety of talents within your group will give it a wonderful vitality of its own!

Nonquilters' Contributions

Are you the only quilter in the group? Your time is certainly of value, but others may also provide some essential elements, including tons of credit and support for your quilting talents!

Some of the things that nonquilters can provide for a group quilt are

- Wishes written in permanent ink on the stars from Neighbor's Fence for a college graduate or sick friend

- Signatures on the hearts from My Heart's Content as a wedding memento or baby-shower gift

- Contributions of money toward fabric and supplies or professional long-arm quilting

- Artwork to be scanned onto fabric and incorporated into your design

- Childcare or a casserole to free you up for completing the project

TABLE RUNNERS

At nearly every retreat I've attended, almost all the women were making something to give away. Why not turn your sewing room into the Studio Gift Shop for a weekend, where creating wonderful gifts is the focus?

Choose cornflowers, ice skates, or sand dollars to appliqué to the basic table-runner pattern. You could also stitch the appliqués onto purchased dish towels, cloth napkins, or place mats for a timesaving, handmade gift that will be enjoyed every day.

CORNFLOWER TABLE RUNNER

SAND DOLLAR TABLE RUNNER

SKATING AWAY TABLE RUNNER

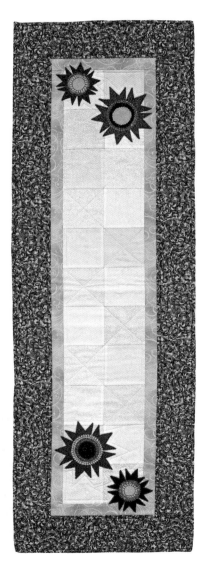  

All table runners designed by Anne Moscicki,
Lake Oswego, Oregon, 2001. Each table runner is 15" x 46½".

BASIC TABLE RUNNER

MATERIALS

6 assorted fat quarters or a variety of assorted light prints at least 4" square for pieced center

¼ yd. for inner border

2 yds. for outer border, backing, and binding

Assorted appliqué fabrics as desired. See photos on pages 37–39 for fabric suggestions.

19" x 52" piece of batting

¾ yd. paper-backed fusible web

2"

Selvages

Fold

Cut 4 binding strips.

CUTTING

From the assorted light prints, cut:
- 22 squares, 4" x 4"

From the inner border fabric, cut:
- 3 strips, 1½" x 42"

From the outer border, backing, and binding fabric, refer to the diagram at upper right and cut:
- 4 strips, 2" x 42", for binding
  Then, referring to the cutting diagram at lower right, open the fabric and cut the remaining pieces:
  - 3 strips, 3½" x 52", for outer border
  - 19" x 52" piece for backing

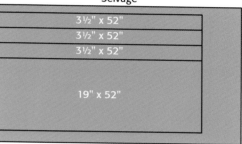

Selvage

3½" x 52"
3½" x 52"
3½" x 52"

19" x 52"

Selvage

Unfold fabric and cut 3 outer border strips and backing.

PIECING THE CENTER

1. Arrange the 22 light print squares into 2 rows of 11 squares each until you are pleased with the distribution of tones and prints.

2. Sew the blocks together into rows. Press the seam allowances in alternate directions.

3. Join the rows, butting the opposing seam allowances together.

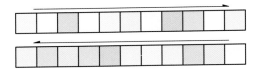

ADDING THE BORDERS

1. For the inner border, add a 1½" x 42" strip to each long side of the pieced center. Trim even with the ends of the pieced center. Press toward the border.

2. Cut the third 1½" x 42" strip in half. Sew a half strip to each short end of the pieced center. Trim the ends even with the inner border on the long sides. Press.

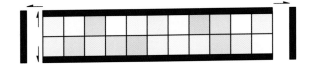

3. For the outer border, add a 3½" x 52" strip to each long side. Trim the ends. Press toward the borders.

4. Cut the third 3½" x 52" strip in half. Sew a half strip to each short end of the pieced center. Trim the ends even with the outer border on the long sides. Press.

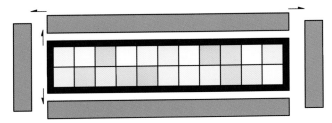

ADDING THE APPLIQUÉS

Trace the appliqué design of your choice from pages 37–39 onto the paper side of the fusible web. Cut slightly beyond the traced line. Press the design, paper side up, to the wrong side of the appliqué fabric according to the fusible web instructions. Cut out the appliqué shapes. Peel off the paper backing and arrange the shapes, fusible side down, onto the table runner. Press. Stitch the appliqué shapes by hand to secure them to the quilt or try using one of your machine's decorative stitches. Refer to "Tips for Decorative Stitching" on page 41.

FINISHING THE TABLE RUNNER

1. Refer to "Quilting Basics" on page 89 as needed to finish your table runner. Prepare the backing, then layer and baste the backing, batting, and table runner together.

2. Quilt as desired or as suggested for each table runner.

3. Trim the excess batting and backing fabric, remove the basting, and bind your table runner. Use the four 2"-wide strips for the binding.

4. Add a label to your table runner.

CORNFLOWER APPLIQUÉS

Add and secure the cornflower appliqués to the pieced table-runner top; then refer to "Finishing the Table Runner." The table runner in the photo has circles quilted within each flower. The pieced area was quilted diagonally through the squares. The outer edge of the inner border was outline quilted.

Arrange petals, forming a pentagonal center.

Layer centers over petals.

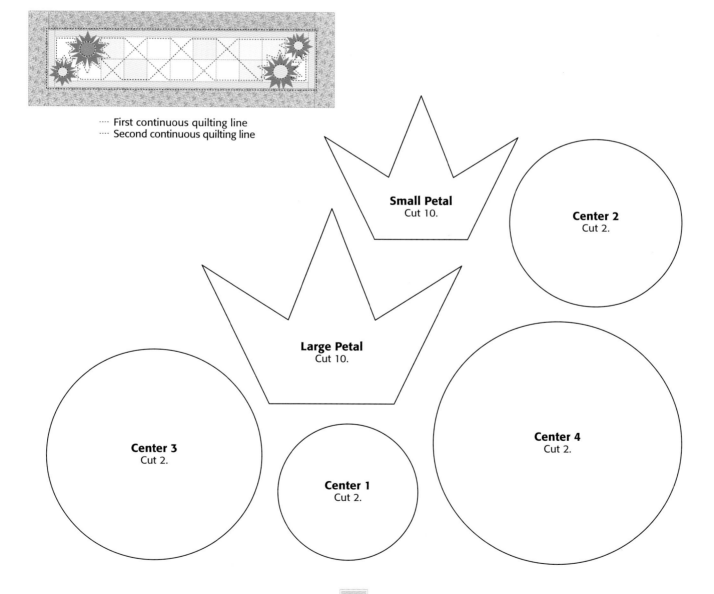

···· First continuous quilting line
···· Second continuous quilting line

Small Petal
Cut 10.

Center 2
Cut 2.

Large Petal
Cut 10.

Center 3
Cut 2.

Center 1
Cut 2.

Center 4
Cut 2.

SAND DOLLAR APPLIQUÉS

Add and secure the sand dollar appliqués to the pieced table-runner top; then refer to "Finishing the Table Runner" on page 36. The table runner in the photo was quilted freehand with several different colors of thread and long, wavy lines to simulate waves lapping onto the shore. The outer edge of the inner border was outline quilted.

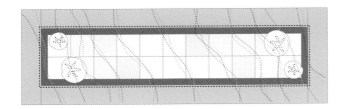

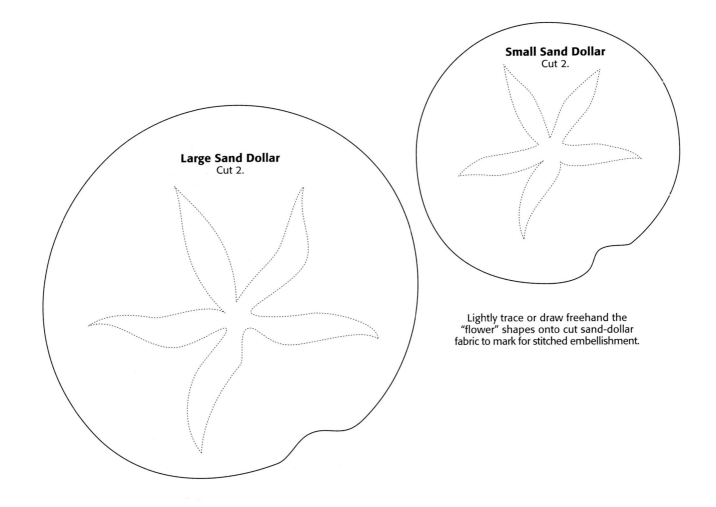

Large Sand Dollar
Cut 2.

Small Sand Dollar
Cut 2.

Lightly trace or draw freehand the "flower" shapes onto cut sand-dollar fabric to mark for stitched embellishment.

Skating Away Appliqués

You will need #8 black perle cotton for the laces on the skates.

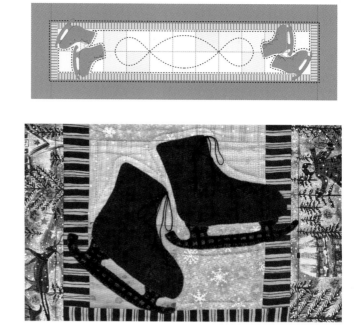

Add and secure the skate appliqués to the pieced table-runner top; then refer to "Finishing the Table Runner." The table runner in the photo was quilted with an elongated "figure-eight" design in the center. Use the edge of your ¼" foot as a guide to evenly outline quilt the skates up to the inner border. Without stopping, continue quilting along the inside of the inner border. Outline quilt on the other side of the inner border seam.

Using black perle cotton, take large stitches as indicated to make the laces, angling your needle as necessary to keep the perle cotton between the layers (rather than on the back). Finish the skates by adding a perle-cotton bow with knotted ends to the top of the laces.

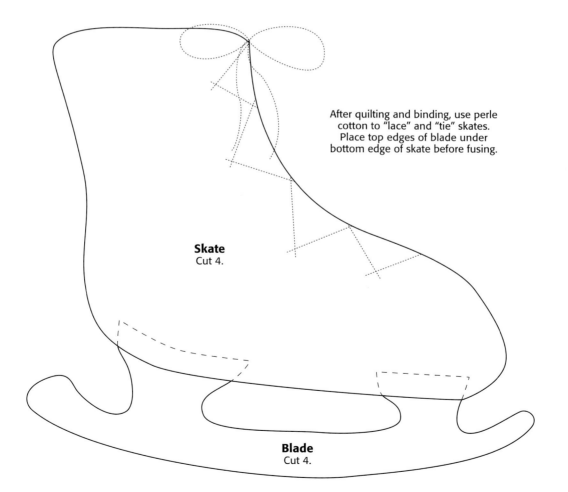

After quilting and binding, use perle cotton to "lace" and "tie" skates. Place top edges of blade under bottom edge of skate before fusing.

Skate
Cut 4.

Blade
Cut 4.

QUICK APPLIQUÉD NAPKINS

For a quick-and-easy gift, stitch the cornflower, sand dollar, or skate appliqués (pages 37–39) onto purchased dish towels, napkins, or place mats. Place the appliqués where they can be seen when the project is used; for example, the corner areas of a place mat or napkin, or centered on one end of a dish towel.

Tips for Decorative Stitching

Loosen up your shoulders and neck, and get ready to have a good time painting with thread!

- Start each project with a test piece that closely resembles your project, perhaps the leftover edges of fused fabric ironed onto a leftover background piece or a trimmed edge of a layered project. This allows you to check the thread colors, adjust the tension, and practice the same curves or angles.

- Go slowly until you get the hang of the particular stitch you've chosen, and slow down again at corners and curves.

- Different threads can add folk-art charm or sophisticated polish. Try them out on scraps to decide the effect that best suits your project.

- Experiment with different thread colors or shades of color that can produce hard edges or soft shading in the finished piece. Try adding dimension by changing to a deeper shade on the "shadow" side of the appliqué.

- Experiment with the stitch width and length; be sure that the foot will accommodate the needle position for a wide stitch.

- Your sewing machine may allow you to change the needle position to the left or right. If so, adjust it to your advantage when stitching on embellishments such as ribbons or to align edges of decorative stitches.

- As you round corners, remember to rotate the entire piece rather than just steering the edge into the sewing machine. Don't fight with the feed dogs!

- When using a decorative stitch, count out the rhythm as the needle goes in and out of the fabric to control your turns and corners. For example, in a leaf-and-flower stitch, you will want to turn after a leaf is completed but before the flower begins.

- Choose a bobbin thread that matches the top thread to lessen the effects of show-through or shading to the top. Adjust machine tension if necessary.

- You may choose to quilt with decorative stitches, but do try out your stitch thoroughly on a test piece. If your walking foot distorts the decorative stitch, consider quilting small projects with your regular foot and lighter weight batting.

Fun and Games

Games and music can help retreat guests who don't know each other well to feel at ease. They can help to start the chatting and get everyone laughing. Ask a retreat guest to take responsibility for bringing the CD player or gathering together the game materials and prizes.

PRIZES

Prizes are fun! A little extra something that you never even knew you wanted can add intrigue to a retreat. You can invite a local quilt shop to provide a prize as small as a discount coupon on a purchase or as luxurious as a gift certificate. You can also plan the cost of prizes into your retreat budget.

Consider asking each person to bring an item to contribute to a prize basket. For example, 12" blocks of the quilter's choice in a specified fabric group would make a great prize. Refer to "Color" on page 32. Equally nice would be a fat-quarter basket in a classic color combination like blues and yellows, or a notions basket filled with the newest gadgets, basics such as rotary blades, or specialty threads.

Another meaningful, no-cost prize can be to extend a little "extra-special" treatment to the winner. For example, the winner or winning team wouldn't have to participate in kitchen cleanup at the end of the day, gets the first shot at the visiting massage therapist, or has coffee and dessert served, compliments of the losing team.

GAMES

Share-and-Tell

Ask each person to bring along something personal to share with the group: a recently finished quilt or photos of quilts she's finished during the past year. You can learn a lot about someone from the quilts she makes and for whom she makes them!

Worst Offender

Give each retreat guest a paper cup or coffee mug with five to ten poker chips or safety pins. Each time an "offense" is committed, take a poker chip away and put it in the kitty. What is an "offense"? At a Learn-to-Quilt workshop, we took chips away whenever we saw a rotary-cutter blade left in the notoriously dangerous open position. It could be uttering a commonly used word, such as *fabric* or *chocolate*, to make the conversation tricky, or bringing up work or household responsibilities while you're on your long-awaited quilting vacation! The guest with the most remaining poker chips wins the prize; if there is a tie for the winner, draw straws.

Miss Congeniality

Take the Worst Offender concept and turn it around to dish up a positive message by giving away poker chips to someone who does something nice: ironing someone else's seams open, warming up coffee, or staying up late to do the dishes. Hold nominations after breakfast on the last morning.

Thief

Each person brings a wrapped notion or fat quarter to the retreat. Each person draws a number from a bowl, and Number One starts out, choosing and opening the wrapped gift that she wants. Now it's Number Two's turn: she may either steal the unwrapped gift from Number One or choose from among the remaining wrapped gifts. If your present is stolen, you get to choose another wrapped gift or become a thief yourself. Limit the number of times a gift can be stolen to two or three to keep the game moving along. This game works best when the gifts are cute and fun rather than meaningful, and when everyone's crafty side comes out!

Quilted Elephant Trade

What's the ugliest fabric or most useless notion you've ever bought? One girl's trash is another's treasure, so disguise it with the most beautiful gift wrap you can and bring it to the Quilted Elephant Trade. Place it secretly in a basket or on a table so no one can connect you to the elephant you've brought. Guests draw numbers from a bowl and choose their new elephant in order. Everyone opens their gifts at once, trying to guess who unearthed this fabulous/hideous item from their stash! Trading is encouraged so that everyone ultimately takes home a treasure. Is anyone up to the challenge of using this new treasure in a project to show off at next year's retreat?

MUSIC

If you have a portable player or your retreat location has one, invite everyone to bring along favorite CDs or tapes. Also, ask them to bring along an open mind about trying some new music. Our annual retreat crosses several generations' worth of musical tastes, ranging from jazz, crooners, and movie soundtracks to classical, rock, and foot-stompin' country. Just about anything goes, as long as the volume isn't making anyone crazy, and after sampling a song or two, anyone should have veto rights. Don't forget to set aside some quiet time, too, although the conversation never seems to stop!

NEIGHBOR'S FENCE

Made up of a variation on a classic Rail Fence block, this quilt couldn't be any easier to piece! It's amazingly versatile: cozy in woodsy flannel prints and plaids, serene in Asian and textured tonal prints, or a real beach party in batiks. Each participant designs her own star to make this quilt shine brightly in any fabric combination. Leftover blocks form a generous buffet runner (page 56) or child's quilt (page 52).

TWIN-SIZE QUILT

BLOCK SIZE: 6"

MATERIALS

Yardage is based on 42"-wide fabric unless otherwise indicated.

16 assorted ¼-yd. pieces for Duo blocks and Trio blocks

8 assorted ⅛-yd. pieces for Trio blocks

½ yd. of gold for stars and cornerstones

½ yd. for inner border

1¼ yds. for outer border

4 yds. for backing

⅝ yd. for binding

Twin-size batting (72" x 84")

¾ yd. paper-backed fusible web

CUTTING

From each ¼-yd. piece, cut:
- 1 strip, 2½" x 42"
- 1 strip, 3½" x 42"

From each ⅛-yd. piece, cut:
- 1 strip, 2½" x 42"

From the gold star fabric, cut:
- 2 strips, 6" x 42"; crosscut into 12 squares, 6" x 6"

From the inner-border fabric, cut:
- 9 strips, 1½" x 42"; crosscut 1 strip into 4 strips, 1½" x 6½"

From the outer-border fabric, cut:
- 6 strips, 6½" x 42"

From the binding fabric, cut:
- 7 strips, 2½" x 42"

MAKING THE NEIGHBOR'S FENCE QUILT ON RETREAT

This pattern divides up nicely for a retreat of seven to twelve people. To make sure that everyone has complete instructions and inspiration, be sure that each participant has a copy of this book.

- Before the retreat, purchase ¾ yard of fabric for the stars. Cut two 6" x 42" strips; then subcut the strips into seven to twelve 6" squares.

- Mail one square to each retreat participant, along with a request for any additional fabrics from their stashes that could be used for borders, binding, or backing. Take the leftover star fabric to the retreat to use in case someone forgets their star. It pays to be prepared!

- Instruct each participant to search her scrap basket or purchase three ¼-yard pieces of fabric in the specified fabric group. (See "Color" on page 32 for tips.) Ask them to make one strip set for the Duo blocks and one strip set for the Trio blocks (page 47).

- Each participant should bring six Duo blocks and six Trio blocks to the retreat, one adorned with a star, and share the sewing and pressing to assemble the blocks into a quilt top.

- Any blocks left over from the group quilt can be used for the Neighbor's Fence Child's Quilt (page 52) or Buffet Runner (page 56).

NEIGHBOR'S FENCE QUILT

A few blocks of island-happy batiks and a sparkly star from every retreat guest grace this simple pattern with the appeal of a tropical getaway.

Designed by Anne Moscicki, Lake Oswego, Oregon, 2002, 62" x 74". Pieced by Denise Bohbot, Laura Evans, Deb Hollister, Sybil Houghton, Karen Martinsson, Kyle McAvoy, Anne Moscicki, Kathy Roethle, Julia Teters, Mimi Teters, Cora Tunberg, and Linda Wyckoff; quilted by Celeste Marshall.

MAKING THE DUO BLOCKS

1. Arrange the 3½"-wide strips into 8 pairs and sew the strips together. Press the seam allowances in either direction.

2. Crosscut each of the strip sets into six 6½" squares until you have at least 40 Duo blocks for the quilt.

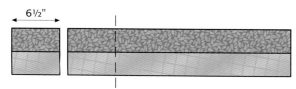

Make 8 strip sets.
Cut 40 Duo blocks.

MAKING THE TRIO BLOCKS

1. Arrange the 2½"-wide strips into 8 sets of 3 strips each. Sew the strips together. Press the seam allowances in either direction.

2. Crosscut each of the strip sets into six 6½" squares until you have at least 40 Trio blocks for the quilt.

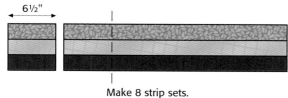

Make 8 strip sets.
Cut 40 Trio blocks.

ADDING THE STARS

1. Choose a dozen of the quilt blocks on which to fuse the stars. They may be either Duo blocks or Trio blocks.

2. Make 12 different star templates by photocopying the pattern on page 49. Mark 2 dots anywhere on the bottom side of the 5½" square, and 1 dot anywhere on each of the 3 remaining sides. Connect the dots to make your own star as shown.

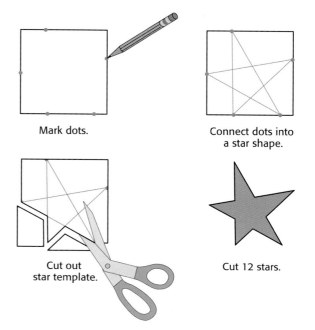

Mark dots.

Connect dots into a star shape.

Cut out star template.

Cut 12 stars.

3. Transfer each design to fusible web by tracing the star shape on the paper side. Cut slightly beyond the traced line of each star. Press each star, paper side up, onto the wrong side of the star fabric according to the fusible web instructions. Cut out the 12 stars on the line. Peel off the paper backing and arrange the stars at jaunty angles on the blocks. Press. Secure the edges with a machine decorative stitch. Refer to "Tips for Decorative Stitching" on page 41.

─────────────

✎ NOTE ✎

It's simpler to add the stars to individual blocks prior to assembling the quilt. If you'd prefer that your stars overlap the block seams as shown on page 50, keep in mind that you'll be working with the entire quilt top as you stitch them on.

ASSEMBLING THE QUILT

1. Lay out all the blocks on a bed or floor, alternating the direction of the Duo blocks and the Trio blocks in a checkerboard pattern. As you lay out the quilt, take time to distribute the stars in a pleasing way.

2. Sew the blocks into rows, pressing all seams toward the Trio blocks to reduce bulk in the finished quilt top. Join the rows, interlocking the block seams. Press the row seams open.

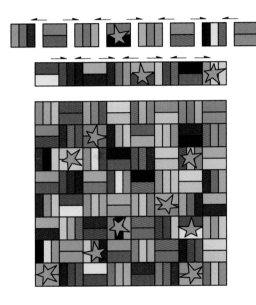

ADDING THE BORDERS

Refer to "Quilting Basics" on pages 89–94 as needed.

1. Measure the quilt from side to side, and then cut the top and bottom outer borders to that measurement.

2. Add one 6½" x 1½" strip of inner border fabric to one side of each cornerstone. Join a cornerstone unit to each end of the top and bottom outer border strips as shown.

3. Measure the quilt from top to bottom and then cut the side inner and outer borders to that measurement. Sew the side inner and outer borders to the quilt.

4. Stitch the top and bottom inner borders to the quilt and trim the ends evenly. Add the top and bottom outer borders, pinning to match the vertical inner-border strips.

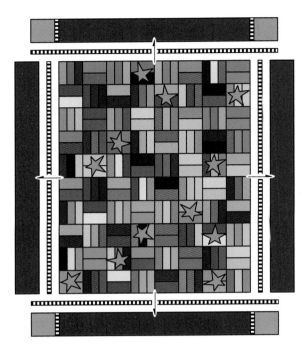

FINISHING THE QUILT

1. Refer to "Quilting Basics" on page 89 as needed to finish your quilt. Prepare the quilt backing; then layer and baste the backing, batting, and quilt top together.

2. Quilt as desired. A lively scrap quilt like this is often best accented with a large, overall design as was used on the quilt in the photo. You could also take inspiration from the stars on the quilt top and try quilting a combination of loops and stars.

3. Trim the excess batting and backing fabric, remove the basting, and bind your quilt. Use the seven 2½"-wide strips for the binding.

4. Add a hanging sleeve if desired. Add a label or pocket to your quilt.

MAKING THE NEIGHBOR'S FENCE QUILT FROM SCRAPS

Lots of different fabrics add depth to this quilt, so it's a great opportunity to clean up your scrap basket or trade with friends!

- Cut 120 rectangles, 2½" x 6½".

- Cut 80 rectangles, 3½" x 6½".

- Pair up the 3½" x 6½" rectangles and stitch to create a total of forty 6½" Duo blocks.

- Stitch three 2½" x 6½" rectangles together. Repeat to create a total of forty 6½" Trio blocks.

Join the blocks as shown in "Assembling the Quilt" on page 48.

Make 1 dot on this side of the box.

Make 1 dot on this side of the box.

Make 1 dot on this side of the box.

Star Pattern

Make 2 dots on this side of the box.

Neighbor's Fence Quilt

Elegant Asian prints, muted colors, and rich textures add serenity and sophistication to the simple blocks of this Neighbor's Fence pattern.

Designed by Anne Moscicki, Lake Oswego, Oregon, 2002, 62" x 74".
Pieced by Anne Moscicki and Linda Wyckoff; quilted by Celeste Marshall.

Auntie's Chocolate Cake

A delicious, tender chocolate cake topped with mocha walnut frosting takes almost no time using this unique recipe. Measure and pack up your dry ingredients in advance to make preparation at the retreat a breeze. Whip it up as soon as you arrive and just leave it out on the counter covered with plastic wrap . . . it will disappear before you pack up to go home!

CHOCOLATE CAKE

2 cups all-purpose flour

1¾ cups sugar

½ teaspoon salt

1 teaspoon baking soda

1 cup (2 sticks) butter or margarine

2 squares (1 ounce each) of semisweet chocolate

1 cup water

2 eggs

½ cup buttermilk

1 teaspoon vanilla

At home:
Combine the flour, sugar, salt, and baking soda in a resealable plastic bag. Label as "Cake."

At the retreat:
Preheat the oven to 350°F. Butter and flour an 11" x 16" x 1" cookie sheet with sides or jelly-roll pan.

In a large saucepan, combine butter, chocolate, and water and heat just until butter and chocolate are melted. Remove from heat and quickly whisk in contents of resealable bag, eggs, buttermilk, and vanilla.

Pour batter into prepared pan. Bake for 25 to 30 minutes, until cake springs back when lightly touched or toothpick comes out clean.

MOCHA WALNUT FROSTING

½ teaspoon salt

1 box (16 ounces) of powdered sugar

1 teaspoon instant espresso powder or instant coffee powder (not granules)

1 cup chopped walnuts

½ cup (1 stick) butter or margarine

2 squares (1 ounce each) of semisweet chocolate

¼ cup milk

1 teaspoon vanilla

At home:
Combine salt, powdered sugar, instant espresso powder or coffee powder, and chopped walnuts in a resealable plastic bag. Label as "Frosting."

At the retreat:
In a medium saucepan, combine butter, chocolate, and milk and stir over low heat just until butter and chocolate are melted. Remove from heat, and while still warm, add vanilla and contents of resealable bag marked "Frosting." Beat well with a wooden spoon. Spread over cake while both cake and frosting are still warm.

CHILD'S QUILT

Depending on the number of people contributing to a Neighbor's Fence group quilt, you may already have enough blocks left over to make the child's quilt. If you're starting from scratch, raid your scrap basket.

Designed by Anne Moscicki, Lake Oswego, Oregon, 2002, 38" x 50". Pieced by Denise Bohbot, Laura Evans, Deb Hollister, Sybil Houghton, Karen Martinsson, Kyle McAvoy, Anne Moscicki, Kathy Roethle, Julia Teters, Mimi Teters, Cora Tunberg, and Linda Wyckoff; quilted by Celeste Marshall.

BLOCK SIZE: 6"

MATERIALS

⅝ yd. total of assorted prints for the Duo blocks and Trio blocks

Scraps, at least 6" square, for as many stars as you'd like to make (optional)

¼ yd. for inner border

⅞ yd. for outer border

1⅝ yds. for backing

⅜ yd. for binding

Crib-size batting (48" x 60")

Paper-backed fusible web (if adding stars)

CUTTING

When this quilt was made on retreat, the borders were created from extra pieces of fabric brought along by the retreat participants, and the cutting sizes of both the inner and outer borders were reduced by ½" to accommodate the available fabrics. Have fun creating your own variations at your retreat or in your own sewing room!

From the assorted prints, cut:
- 36 rectangles, 2½" x 6½"
- 24 rectangles, 3½" x 6½"

From the inner border fabric, cut:
- 4 strips, 1½" x 42"

From the outer border fabric, cut:
- 4 strips, 6½" x 42"

From the binding fabric, cut:
- 5 strips, 2½" x 42"

MAKING THE BLOCKS

1. For each Duo block, pair up 3½" x 6½" rectangles. Stitch the rectangles together to make a total of twelve 6½" Duo blocks. Refer to the block construction for the Neighbor's Fence quilt on page 47.

2. For each Trio block, stitch three 2½" x 6½" rectangles together. Make a total of twelve 6½" Trio blocks.

3. If you are adding stars to the child's quilt, follow the instructions for the Neighbor's Fence quilt on page 47.

ASSEMBLING THE CHILD'S QUILT AND BORDERS

1. Lay out the blocks and arrange them until you are pleased with the distribution of color and prints.

2. Sew the blocks into rows, pressing the seams toward the Duo blocks. Join the rows, interlocking the block seams. Press the row seams open.

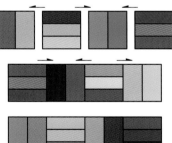

3. Add the inner and outer borders as described in "Quilting Basics" on page 89.

FINISHING THE QUILT

1. Refer to "Quilting Basics" on page 89 as needed to finish your quilt. To prepare the backing for the Neighbor's Fence child's quilt, simply press the backing fabric free of any wrinkles. It will not need any piecing. Layer and baste the backing, batting, and quilt top together.

2. Quilt as desired.

3. Trim the excess batting and backing fabric, remove the basting, and bind your quilt. Use the five 2½"-wide strips for the binding.

4. Add a hanging sleeve if desired. Add a label or pocket to your quilt.

The Pleasure of Your Company Is Requested…

An inviting invitation sets the tone for the weekend in addition to providing basic information everyone will need. To get participants excited about coming, use clip art or photographs, find a quilt-themed note card, stitch along the edge of the card or stationery (leaving an inch or so of thread ends dangling), or enclose stickers, purchased or printed, that invitees can place on personal calendars to block out the days for quilting and good friends. If you and your buddies are wired, email links to Web sites for the town, hotel, or rental property where you'll be staying, or send links for all the quilt shops you'll pass on the way to your destination!

Send invitations at least two months in advance so that everyone can block out time in their busy lives. Don't forget to include dates; check-in and check-out times; the full cost, the person who must receive it, and the due date; a basic itinerary; and who to call or email with questions. Also ask for any help you'll need with tasks such as food preparation (noting any dietary restrictions that need to be accommodated), cost tracking, and driving. If you're creating a group quilt, briefly inform participants of their responsibilities in contributing to it. For an example of how to pull all this information together, take a look at the sample flyer on the facing page.

Once you know who's coming, use a follow-up letter to provide a packing list, directions, a phone number for emergencies, and complete information about the group quilt.

It's time to retreat!

Join us June 15–17 at a beautiful beach house in Bear Paw Juction, USA, for a weekend of quilting, music, and great food. We can't wait to see you!

We've enclosed a pattern for the fun and easy retreat quilt. You'll purchase ¾ yard of fabric and make your blocks before the retreat. Each of us will donate twenty minutes at the retreat to put the blocks together. Please bring your suggestions for a charity or organization that will benefit from our efforts.

A $75 fee covers lodging, food, and the cost of having the retreat quilt professionally finished (we'll refund any extra money). If you'd like to indulge in the services of the massage therapist we've invited, you'll need to pay an additional fee directly to her, with cash or check. And you'll need some cash for a lunch out on Saturday, as well as for any optional treks to the local quilt shop.

See you there!

Send your check and sign-up sheet to:

Susie Nine Patch
1234 Rotary Row
Sawtooth City, USA   55555

Any questions?

Contact Janet Pinwheel at mail@ourquiltingretreat.com or 123-555-1234.

Yes! Sign me up . . . I need to retreat!

Name _____

_____ Enclosed is my check for $75.00

_____ Sign me up for a massage! *(Bring cash or a check to pay the massage therapist directly.)*

_____ ½ hour _____1 hour _____15 minute neck & shoulders

Do you need a ride? _____ Yes _____ No

Can you bring another person in your car? _____ Yes _____No

Can you transport things like extra tables? _____ Yes _____ No

BUFFET RUNNER

This oversized table runner is large enough to handle a full buffet. Depending on the number of people contributing to a Neighbor's Fence group quilt, you may already have enough blocks left over to make the buffet runner. If you're starting from scratch, schedule an afternoon with a friend and make two or more buffet runners, sharing the contents of your scrap baskets!

Designed by Anne Moscicki, Lake Oswego, Oregon, 2002, 26" x 80".
Pieced by Anne Moscicki and Linda Wyckoff; quilted by Celeste Marshall.

MATERIALS

⅝ yd. total of assorted prints for the Duo blocks and Trio blocks

1 scrap, at least 6" square, for each star (optional)

¼ yd. for inner border

1⅛ yds. for outer border

2½ yds. for backing

⅝ yd. for binding

30" x 84" piece of batting

Fusible web (if adding stars)

CUTTING

From the assorted prints, cut:
- 33 rectangles, 2½" x 6½"
- 22 rectangles, 3½" x 6½"

From the inner border fabric, cut:
- 5 strips, 1½" x 42"

From the outer border fabric, cut:
- 6 strips, 6½" x 42"

From the binding fabric, cut:
- 6 strips, 2½" x 42"

ASSEMBLING THE BLOCKS

1. For each block, pair up 3½" x 6½" rectangles. Stitch the rectangles together to make a total of eleven 6½" Duo blocks. Refer to the block construction in the Neighbor's Fence quilt on page 47.

2. For each block, stitch three 2½" x 6½" rectangles together. Make a total of eleven 6½" Trio blocks.

3. If you are adding stars to the buffet runner, follow the instructions in the Neighbor's Fence quilt on page 47.

ASSEMBLING THE BUFFET RUNNER

1. Lay out the blocks and arrange them until you are pleased with the distribution of color and prints.

2. Sew the blocks into rows, pressing the seams in alternate directions. Join the rows, interlocking the seams.

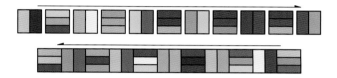

3. Add the inner and outer borders as described in "Quilting Basics" on page 89.

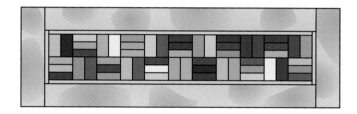

FINISHING THE BUFFET RUNNER

1. Refer to "Quilting Basics" on page 89 as needed to finish your quilt. To prepare the backing for the buffet runner, simply press the backing fabric free of any wrinkles. It will not need any piecing. Layer and baste the backing, batting, and quilt top together.

2. Quilt as desired.

3. Trim the excess batting and backing fabric, remove the basting, and bind your quilt. Use the six 2½"-wide strips for the binding.

4. Add a label or pocket to your quilt.

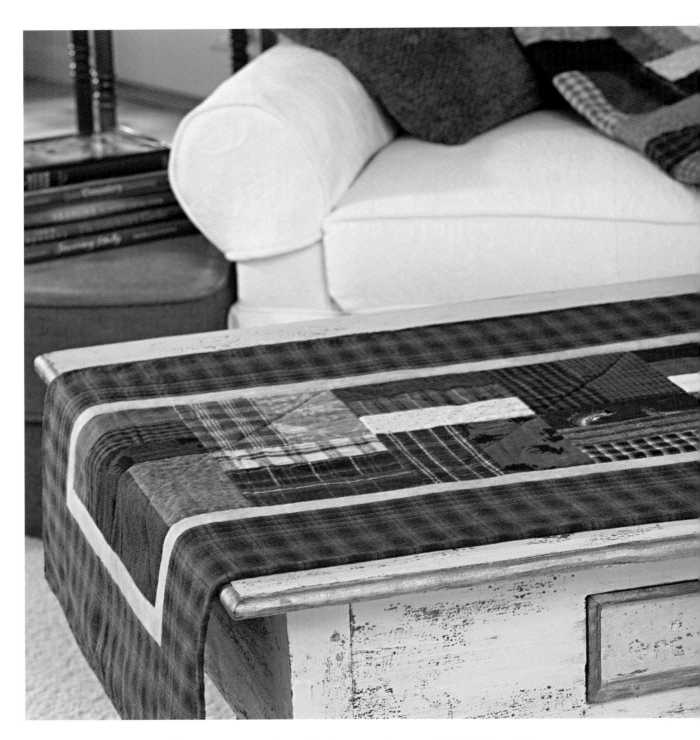

Designed by Anne Moscicki, Lake Oswego, Oregon, 2002, 26" x 80".
Pieced and quilted by Linda Wyckoff.

NEIGHBORS' FENCE
BUFFET RUNNER AND QUILT

Simple Neighbor's Fence blocks turn rugged flannel plaids and prints into a warm quilt or a table runner that adds high-country charm to any room. Grab your scrap basket and refer to pages 45–57.

Designed by Anne Moscicki,
Lake Oswego, Oregon, 2002, 62" x 74".
Pieced by Linda Wyckoff and Anne
Moscicki; quilted by Celeste Marshall.

SCRAP SOUP

Bon appétit! This quilt is named for the everything-into-the-pot soup that has become our annual retreat's traditional first-night meal. Too many cooks can't spoil this quilt; the more lively food prints, the better!

Scrap Soup Quilt

BLOCK SIZE: 6"

Materials

Yardage is based on 42"-wide fabric unless otherwise indicated. In collecting fabric for this quilt, pair each food print with a bright coordinate.

8 assorted fat quarters of large-scale fruit, vegetable, or other food prints

8 assorted fat quarters of bright coordinating prints

1¼ yds. of red print for pinwheels and inner border

1½ yds. for outer border and binding

3¾ yds. for backing

66" x 66" piece of batting

RETREAT TIP

This quilt is perfect for a group of eight to make. The organizer should purchase the red fabric for the pinwheels and inner border. Cut it and send two 7¼" red squares to each participant. Each participant should have a copy of this book. They should also purchase one fat quarter each of a food print and a coordinating print. Using the red squares, everyone makes four Pinwheel blocks and four Triangle blocks. Ask them to save all the scraps to make the "chopped" border. Get together for a weekend or an evening to square up and join the blocks, and enjoy one another's company!

Cutting

Referring to the diagrams, cut the fat quarters into three 6⅞" squares, one 7¼" square, and strips for the chopped border. Keep each set of food print squares and coordinating print squares paired throughout the assembly process.

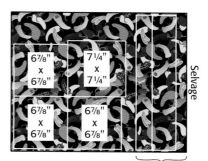

Cut 2 to 3 strips, varying from 2" to 3" wide.

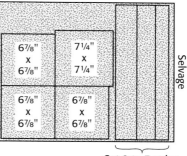

Cut 2 to 3 strips, varying from 2" to 3" wide.

From the red print, cut:
- 4 strips, 7¼" x 42"; crosscut into 16 squares, 7¼" x 7¼"
- 5 strips, 1½" x 42"

From the outer border and binding fabric, cut:
- 6 strips, 4½" x 42"
- 7 strips, 2½" x 42"

SCRAP SOUP QUILT

A vivid array of fruit, vegetable, and prepared-food prints is gathered into a mélange of half-square triangles accented with red-pepper pinwheels.

Designed by Anne Moscicki, Lake Oswego, Oregon, 2001, 60" x 60".
Pieced by Linda Wyckoff and Anne Moscicki; quilted by Celeste Marshall.

ASSEMBLING THE TRIANGLE BLOCKS

Use two 6⅞" squares each from a food print and a coordinating fabric to make these half-square triangles. Reserve the remaining 6⅞" square of each to make the Pinwheel blocks.

1. With right sides together, layer one 6⅞" food print square with one 6⅞" coordinating square.

2. Draw a line diagonally from corner to corner on the lighter square.

3. Sew ¼" from the line on both sides and then cut on the line.

4. Press the seam allowances toward the darker fabric. Repeat to make a total of 32 Triangle blocks.

Triangle Block
Make 32.

ASSEMBLING THE PINWHEEL BLOCKS

1. With right sides together, layer one 7¼" food print or coordinating square with one 7¼" red square.

2. Draw a line diagonally from corner to corner on the lighter square.

3. Sew ¼" from the line on both sides and then cut on the line.

4. Press the seam allowances toward the darker fabric. Trim each block to 6⅞". Repeat to make a total of 16 blocks.

Make 16.

5. With right sides together, layer 1 Pinwheel block with 1 of the reserved 6⅞" squares of the food print or coordinating fabric.

6. Draw a line diagonally from corner to corner on the plain square.

7. Sew ¼" from the line on both sides and then cut on the line.

8. Press the seam allowances toward the large triangle. Trim each block to 6½". Repeat to make a total of 32 blocks.

Pinwheel Block
Make 32.

ASSEMBLING THE CHOPPED BORDER

1. Sew the strips cut from the fat quarters together into sets. You will need a total of 4 sets, each at least 15" wide. Press the seams open.

2. Cut four 2½" x 15" segments from each strip set.

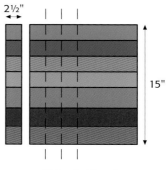

Make 4 strip sets.
Cut 4 segments from each set.

3. Arrange the segments into groups of 4. Stitch them together into 4 long pieced border strips. Press.

Make 4.

ASSEMBLING THE QUILT AND BORDERS

1. Taking note of the quilt plan, arrange the Triangle and Pinwheel blocks. Just as every creative cook will add her own special touch to a recipe, your quilt may not follow the plan precisely. Just focus on creating the 8 red Pinwheel blocks and distributing the colors and prints in a pleasing array in the alternate blocks. Notice that the large triangles within each Pinwheel block fall randomly, adding movement throughout the quilt. Sew the pieced blocks into 8 rows. Press the row seams in alternate directions.

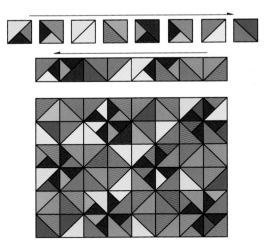

2. Add the inner border as described in "Quilting Basics" on page 89.

3. Add the chopped border strips to the sides and then to the top and bottom of the quilt. Open the seams to remove extra pieces, or trim to fit.

4. Add the 4½"-wide outer border as described in "Quilting Basics" on page 89.

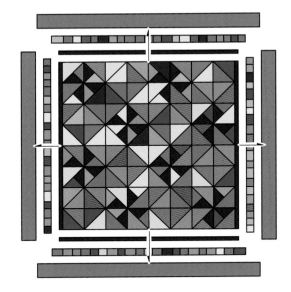

FINISHING THE QUILT

1. Refer to "Quilting Basics" on page 89 as needed to finish your quilt. Prepare the quilt backing, then layer and baste the backing, batting, and quilt top together.

2. Quilt as desired. In the pictured quilt, a medium stipple in green thread was used on the entire quilt except for the red pinwheels; these were quilted with a small stipple in red thread. Each of the uneven segments in the chopped border was quilted corner to corner, creating a funky zigzag.

3. Trim the excess batting and backing fabric, remove the basting, and bind your quilt. Use the seven 2½"-wide strips for the binding.

4. Add a hanging sleeve if desired. Add a label or pocket to your quilt.

BREAD-BASKET WARMER

Use leftover blocks from your Scrap Soup group quilt to make this cheery bread-basket warmer, or make a single block from the directions here. The rice-filled center of the bread-basket warmer heats in the microwave, then tucks into the bottom of the bread basket to keep bread warm throughout your meal.

FINISHED SIZE: 18" x 18"

MATERIALS

Yardage is based on 42"-wide fabric unless otherwise indicated.

4 squares, 5⅜" x 5⅜", of red for Pinwheel block

4 squares, 5⅜" x 5⅜", of assorted prints for Pinwheel block

4 squares, 7¼" x 7¼", of assorted prints for outer triangles

2 squares, 9⅞" x 9⅞", of green print for border triangles

20" x 20" square for backing

7¼" x 7¼" square for pocket on back

2 squares, 6" x 6", of muslin for rice bag

1 cup rice

¼ yd. for binding

20" x 20" piece of batting

Front   Back

CUTTING

From the 7¼" outer-triangle prints, cut:
- each square in half diagonally for a total of 8 triangles; you will use one of each print

From the 9⅞" green print, cut:
- each square in half diagonally for a total of 4 triangles

From the binding fabric, cut:
- two 2" x 42" strips

PIECING THE PINWHEEL BLOCK

1. With right sides together, layer one 5⅜" red square with one 5⅜" print square.

2. Draw a line diagonally from corner to corner on the lighter square. Sew on the line and then cut ¼" from the line.

3. Press the seam allowance toward the red triangle.

4. Repeat to make 3 more half-square-triangle units. Stitch the 4 units into a Pinwheel block.

Make 1.

5. With right sides together, layer one 7¼" outer triangle over the Pinwheel block as shown, aligning the long edge of the triangle with the Pinwheel block edge. The triangle points should evenly overhang the sides of the Pinwheel block. Sew the seam and press it toward the outer triangle.

6. Sew an outer triangle to the opposite side of the Pinwheel block. Repeat with the remaining 2 triangles to complete the block.

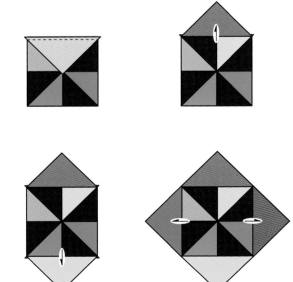

ADDING THE BORDER TRIANGLES

1. With right sides together, layer 1 border triangle over the Pinwheel block. Sew the seam and press it toward the border triangle.

2. Sew a border triangle to the opposite side of the block. Repeat with the remaining 2 triangles to complete the block.

QUILTING THE BREAD BASKET WARMER

1. Refer to "Quilting Basics" on page 89 as needed to finish your bread-basket warmer.

2. Quilt as desired. The bread-basket warmer pictured was quilted around the red pinwheel shape using black topstitch thread and a decorative stitch (refer to "Decorative Stitching Tips" on page 41). The edges of the pieced block were quilted with matching thread ¼" from the edge.

3. Trim the excess batting and backing fabric, remove the basting, and bind the bread basket warmer.

18"

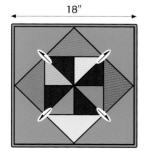
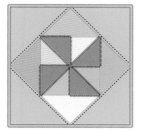

MAKING THE RICE PILLOW

1. Layer the two 6" muslin squares and sew around all 4 edges with a ¼" seam, leaving a 3" opening along one side. Turn the bag right side out and press.

2. Using a funnel, fill the pillow with 1 cup of rice.

3. Pin the 3" opening closed and topstitch ⅛" from the edge on all 4 sides to finish the rice pillow.

ADDING THE POCKET

1. Hem the edges of the 7¼" pocket square by folding in ¼" on all sides. Repeat for a double hem. Stitch ⅛" away from the folded edges.

2. Position the pocket in the center back of the quilted bread-basket warmer.

3. Secure the pocket by hand sewing on 3 sides only. Be sure to catch only the backing fabric so that the stitches don't show from the front.

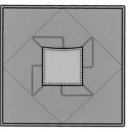

Use the quilting lines on the back as a guide for pocket placement.

USING THE BREAD-BASKET WARMER

Warm the rice bag in the microwave for one to two minutes, stopping the microwave once or twice during heating to redistribute the rice and check for excessive temperature. Place the warm rice bag into the pocket on the back of the bread-basket warmer. Place your warm bread or muffins into the basket, folding the corners of the bread-basket warmer over the top to keep your bread warm throughout the meal.

Scrap Soup

This hearty vegetarian soup paired with a loaf of great bread has become a first-night staple at our retreats. Preparing the vegetables before you leave saves lots of time later. As soon as you arrive at your destination, place everything but the salt and pepper in a large pot and set to simmer. As you unpack and set up your quilting, the house will fill with a savory aroma to welcome your friends!

SCRAP SOUP

2 tablespoons olive oil

1 medium yellow onion, chopped

2 cloves garlic, minced

3 stalks celery, sliced

8 medium carrots, peeled (if desired) and sliced

2 russet potatoes, peeled (if desired) and chopped to a 1" dice

1 bag (10 ounces) prewashed and trimmed spinach

1½ cups frozen corn

1½ cups frozen peas

1 can (26 ounces) chopped tomatoes

2 cans (8 ounces) vegetable juice, such as V-8

1 can (14 ounces) garbanzo beans, drained

Salt and pepper

At home:

Prepare onion, garlic, celery, carrots, potatoes, and spinach and place in resealable bags. Store in refrigerator. Measure frozen peas and corn and place them in a resealable bag. Store in freezer.

At the retreat:

Heat oil in a large saucepan over medium heat. Add onion and sauté until golden. Add garlic and celery and sauté for a few more minutes, taking care not to burn garlic. Add remaining ingredients (except the salt and pepper) and simmer until vegetables are tender. Salt and pepper to taste.
Serves 10.

Variations

- If you prefer stew to soup, omit 1 can (15 ounce) of vegetable juice.

- If you prefer nonvegetarian stew, add 1 pound of sautéed ground beef or turkey, or 2 to 3 cups of cooked, shredded chicken.

- You may choose to roast the chopped onion, sliced carrots, and diced potatoes to bring out rich, robust flavors. Preheat oven to 425°F. Place the vegetables and 1 additional tablespoon of olive oil in a glass baking dish and toss to coat the vegetables with the oil. Salt and pepper them lightly. Arrange the vegetables in a single layer. Place the dish in the oven and roast for 30 to 45 minutes, stirring them once or twice, until vegetables are fork-tender and edges are brown. Cool and place in a resealable bag, and then store in the refrigerator up to 2 days before placing them in the soup. Note that roasting the vegetables will reduce the soup cooking time.

COTTAGE SPA

Part traditional
whole-cloth quilt,
part favorite chenille
bathrobe, this quilt
is a perfect blend
of simplicity and
luxury in an easy,
elegant quilt.
Simple geometric
quilting makes it
a quick project, or
show off fine quilting
designs on a palette
of beautiful fabric.

Cottage Spa Throw

Treat yourself to all the indulgences of a spa at home, including this throw made with luxuriously textured fabrics.

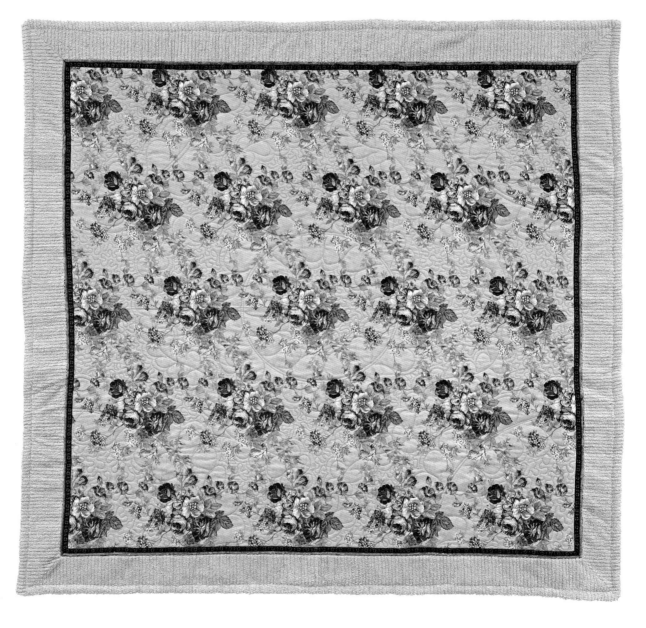

Designed and pieced by Anne Moscicki, Lake Oswego, Oregon, 2002, 60" x 60"; quilted by Celeste Marshall.

COTTAGE SPA THROW

MATERIALS

Note the different fabric widths required for this project.

1¾ yds. of 54"-wide fabric for center (main fabric)

¾ yd. of 72"-wide chenille for border

4 yds. of 42"-wide muslin for lining★

2 yds. of 72"-wide chenille for backing

7 yds. of ½"-wide decorative ribbon

7 yds. of ¼"-wide velvet piping with ¼" edge for seam allowance

68" x 68" piece of batting

★*Muslin will be cut into two 72" segments.*

CUTTING

From the main fabric, cut:
∾ 1 square, 52" x 52"

From the chenille border fabric, cut:
∾ 4 strips, 5" x 72"

From the ribbon and piping, cut:
∾ 4 pieces of each, 60" long

ASSEMBLING THE QUILT

1. With right sides together, position a chenille border strip against one edge of the main fabric, allowing about 6" of the border strip to extend beyond both edges of the main fabric. Sew, beginning and ending the seam ¼" from the edge of the main fabric. Press the seam allowance toward the chenille border. Repeat to add the chenille border strip to the opposite side of the main fabric.

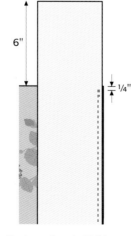

6"

¼"

Begin and end stitching ¼" from edge of main fabric.

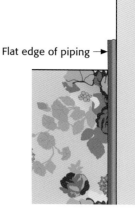

Flat edge of piping →

2. Working from the front, position the rolled edge of the piping next to the chenille border, with the flat piping edge facing toward the center. There should be approximately 2" of piping extending beyond the main fabric.

3. Position the ribbon over the seam allowance edge of the piping. There should be approximately 2" of ribbon extending beyond the main fabric.

4. Stitch both edges of the ribbon to secure both the piping and the ribbon. You may find it helpful to replace the presser foot with a zipper foot or adjust the needle position to the left or right to accommodate the piping as you sew. Begin and end the seam ¼" from the edge of the main fabric. Trim the ribbon even with the edge of the main fabric, but leave the piping tail as is. Bring the thread ends through to the back of the quilt and tie them off.

5. Center and stitch a chenille border strip to the top and bottom of the main fabric, beginning and ending the seam ¼" from the edge of the main fabric.

6. Position the piping and ribbon along the top and bottom main-fabric edge. At the corners, fold the flat piping edge under the piping, and

allow the tails to tuck behind the overlapping border strips.

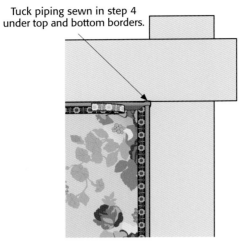

Tuck piping sewn in step 4 under top and bottom borders.

Fold flat piping edge under piping and tuck behind overlapping chenille border.

7. Turn the top layer of ribbon back at a 45-degree angle and tuck under the piping. Trim the excess; pin and stitch into place.

8. Bring the thread ends through to the back of the quilt and tie them off.

MITERING THE BORDERS

Because of the bulk of the chenille, use a walking foot for this step.

1. Lay the quilt flat. Fold 1 chenille border strip under, creating a 45-degree angle. Pin into position before you press the fold.

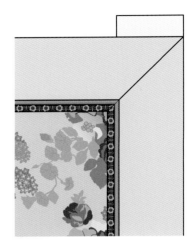

2. Fold the quilt top so that the borders are parallel, with the quilt center folded at a 45-degree angle. Note the crease and check its angle with your ruler. Adjust as necessary and pin the borders into place.

3. Stitch from the inside of the border to the outer border edge directly on the crease, stitching over the piping tails. Trim the piping tails to approximately 1".

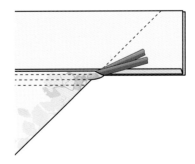

4. Open to check the results. If you're satisfied, trim the excess chenille a generous ¼" from the seam line. Press the seams open.

5. Repeat for the remaining 3 corners.

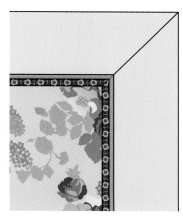

QUILTING THE THROW

1. Cut the muslin in half to make two 72" segments. Remove the selvage on one side of each piece. Seam those edges together to create the lining. Press the seam open.

2. Refer to "Quilting Basics" on page 89 as needed. Layer and baste the lining, batting, and front of throw together.

3. Quilt the main-fabric area but do not quilt the borders. Fill the space simply and elegantly with a simple geometric design, or showcase a beautiful medallion design or other favorite motif.

FINISHING THE THROW

1. Place the backing chenille, right side up, on a large work surface. Smooth it and hold it in place with tape or pins.

2. With right sides together, lay the quilted top over it. Smooth the quilted top, and working from the center out, pin as necessary to prevent wrinkling. Pin the chenille borders to the chenille backing through the lining and batting layers.

3. Trim away the excess backing.

4. Stitch the edges with a ½"-wide seam allowance, leaving 24" open on one side. Clip the corners at an angle to reduce bulk.

5. Turn the quilt right side out, pushing the corners square with a chopstick or other blunt tip. Hand stitch the opening closed.

6. Pin the border edges, keeping the outer seam even. Using your walking foot, stitch around the border ½" from the edge.

7. If desired, tie the chenille backing to the quilted center of your Cottage Spa Throw.

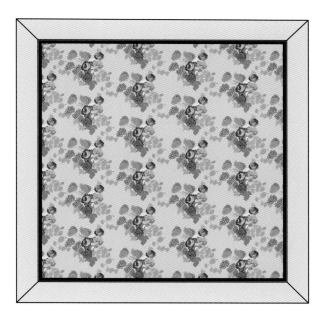

ENVELOPE PURSE

These charming little purses hold jewelry, scarves, wedding keepsakes—anything special! Fill them with homemade spa indulgences for a thoughtful gift. This pattern makes two 7" x 6½" purses. You can use the same method to create larger or smaller variations.

MATERIALS

Yardage is based on 42"-wide fabric unless otherwise indicated. Materials are enough for two purses.

1 fat quarter for purse exterior

1 fat quarter for purse interior

18" x 22" piece of batting

¼ yd. for binding

Tassels, ribbons, decorative thread for machine stitching, or other embellishment

Snaps, Velcro, buttons, or other closures

ASSEMBLING THE PURSES

1. Layer the batting between the wrong sides of the fabrics. Baste, pin, or spray-baste to hold the layers together.

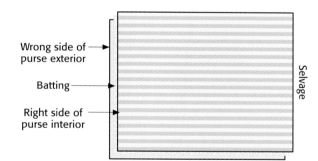

2. Quilt as desired. Cut the quilted fabrics into two 7" x 18" pieces.

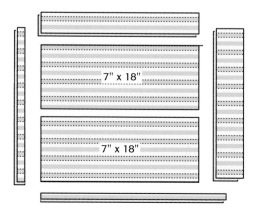

3. At one end, you may choose to trim the corners at a 45-degree angle, measuring 1" to 2" from the corner as shown below. Or you might want to round the corners, tracing a jar lid or saucer to keep a consistent shape, or you could leave the corners squared.

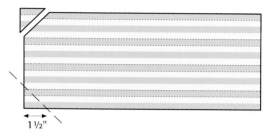

4. Cut two 2"-wide strips for the binding and join the strips end to end to form one long strip. Bind the bottom edge of the purse, referring to "Adding the Binding" on pages 92–94 as needed. Trim the excess binding even with the edge of the quilted fabrics. Add decorative stitching around the remaining edges, if desired. Measure the width of the stitch and mark the quilted purse shape, keeping the binding width in mind. Avoid stitching too close to the edge; you don't want the binding added in step 6 to cover it.

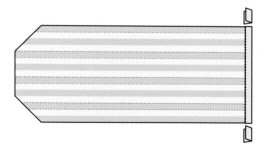

5. Fold the bottom edge up 6½"; pin the sides.

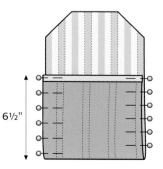

6. If you've chosen to add a tassel, pin it in place. Working on the exterior side, stitch the binding to the remaining edges, leaving 1" or more excess binding at both the beginning and end. Pin tassels in place if desired.

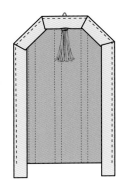

7. Trim the beginning and ending binding about ⅜" to ½" from the folded bottom edge of the purse. Fold the cut ends up and inside the binding as you hand stitch the binding into place.

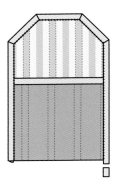

8. Add decorative buttons, buttons and button-holes, or other embelllishments as desired to personalize your purse.

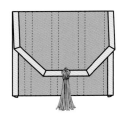

A spa visit awaits you in the comfort of your own home! Try these simple indulgences to rejuvenate yourself, or make some up as gifts for a harried friend and tuck them into an envelope purse along with an inspiring poem or thought.

OLIVE OIL AND SEA SALT SCRUB

Gently rub small amounts into feet, elbows, and hands to soften, moisturize, and remove dry skin.

- ½ cup sea salt
- ¼ cup olive oil or scented massage oil

1. In a small bowl, mix the salt and oil to a paste.
2. Heat the mixture in the microwave to warm, heating in small increments to keep the mixture from getting dangerously hot. Stir before testing temperature.
3. Gently rub into skin.
4. Rinse with warm water.
5. Store in the refrigerator for up to 2 weeks.

LAVENDER BATH TEA

Place this bath tea bag into your tub as it fills for a fragrant, relaxing bath. Lavender calms the nerves and oatmeal soothes the skin.

- 1 teaspoon dried lavender buds
- 2 teaspoons regular rolled oats
- 8" square of cheesecloth or muslin
- String or perle cotton

1. Lay cheesecloth flat. Place lavender and oatmeal in center and mix lightly with your fingers.
2. Bring the ends of the cheesecloth or muslin together and tie with string or perle cotton.

NOTE: *Before using any skin-care product, do a small patch test to make sure that it won't irritate your skin.*

Luxurious Additions

Hiring a Teacher

Hiring a talented instructor is a great idea if everyone is interested in learning or refining a technique. The class could feature curved piecing or a challenging pattern, such as a Feathered Star or Mariner's Compass.

℞ Start by talking with a teacher whose classes you've enjoyed, or ask for recommendations from the staff at your favorite quilt shop or at a shop close to your retreat destination.

℞ Talk with the instructor in person, if possible, and get to know her a bit; she will be sharing accommodations with you for the weekend!

℞ Discuss accommodations and give her copies of the invitation and follow up with her so that she will know the tone of your weekend.

℞ Offer her a private bedroom, include her as a friend, and expect to pay for her meals.

℞ Formulate a simple contract for the participants, stating dates, fees, and a deposit due date.

Hiring a Helper

A helper can be a nice person to have around when you realize that your Feathered Star calls for over one thousand 2" half-square triangles! This is a real lifesaver if you have decided as a group to tackle a complex pieced pattern, or if finished projects are a serious goal. A good helper will press and square up, and a great helper will also warm up your cup of coffee and smile the whole time!

℞ Where do you begin to look for an angel like this? Be forewarned that she may not be easy to find! Someone's teenage daughter may enjoy being included, or call the quilt shop nearest to your destination and ask if a staff member might like to earn extra money.

℞ Talk to your potential helpers and get to know them. Look for someone cheerful and friendly, and try to decide if her personality will fit with your mix of friends and will create no impediment to your conversations.

℞ Pay her well, and tip generously for a good job, but expect to pay her with more than just money; somebody willing to do your grunt work and continue to smile deserves serious appreciation and praise.

℞ Make sure that her time is evenly split among those who want to avail themselves of her services; using a sign-up sheet will keep things fair. Remember to schedule breaks and personal time!

INDULGING IN A MASSAGE THERAPIST

Aaaah! This is the life! A great massage is a true body-and-soul experience that will leave you both relaxed and energized. You can request short (fifteen-minute) massages of neck, arms, and shoulders, usually done in a chair rather than lying on a table. This type of massage does not require clothing removal, so nobody has to be shy. For a totally "aaahhhh" experience, a half-hour or full-hour massage with a good massage therapist can't be matched; this weekend is for body, soul, and quilting, so indulge! If you or other participants have never enjoyed a massage, ask the massage therapist to start gently and build to comfortable pressure. After spending hours at your machine, you will feel fabulous!

- When you reserve your retreat location, contact the local Chamber of Commerce or a nearby day spa for a licensed massage therapist to visit you at the retreat.

- Specify a female massage therapist if you feel your guests will be more comfortable.

- Ask your retreat guests to sign up, in advance, for the length of massage that they would like so your massage therapist can schedule enough time to handle the whole group.

- Each person will pay the massage therapist directly, so find out what types of payment are acceptable and let each person in the group know.

- It's appropriate to tip the massage therapist a few extra dollars if you've enjoyed her services.

- Occasionally, a spa may want to charge an additional fee to send a massage therapist to you. Qualified, licensed massage therapists who are not employed by a spa exclusively are usually willing to come to you without additional charges, so shop around.

- Be prepared to offer your massage therapist a quiet room where she won't be disturbed as she works. Your massage therapist will bring her own massage chair or table and often some relaxing music. She will need to schedule time to set up and break down her equipment.

- Your massage therapist may also offer specialty lotions or other products for sale. If so, ask her to set them in an area where everyone can see or sample them and decide for themselves. No sales pitches, please!

BEST FRIENDS

One of the first quilts my sister Julia taught me to sew was a Flying Geese variation. Though there are many variations for setting the Flying Geese blocks, this one reminds me of the give-and-take approach that best friends—and sisters—are famous for. Leftover blocks stitch together so you can fill them with pungent pine needles or soothing lavender to make sweet sachets. Tuck them into a suitcase, or hang them in your closet.

BEST FRIENDS QUILT

Friendships can make your spirits soar! This setting for the classic Flying Geese block echoes the give-and-take approach for which best friends are famous.

Designed by Anne Moscicki, Lake Oswego, Oregon, 2001, 48" x 56".
Pieced by Cindy Pope and Anne Moscicki; quilted by Celeste Marshall.

LAP QUILT

BLOCK SIZE: 3" x 6"

MATERIALS

Yardage is based on 42"-wide fabric unless otherwise indicated.

⅝ yd. *each* of 12 dark fabrics for "geese" and sashing

1⅜ yds. total of assorted light fabrics for block backgrounds

3⅜ yds. for backing

⅝ yd. for binding

55" x 61" piece of batting

CUTTING

From each *dark fabric, cut:*
- 1 square, 13¼" x 13¼"; crosscut diagonally in both directions to yield 4 triangles from each fabric
- 1 square, 6⅞" x 6⅞"; crosscut diagonally in half to yield 2 triangles from each fabric
- 1 strip, 3½" x 42"; crosscut into 6 rectangles, 3½" x 6½"

From the assorted light prints cut:
- 12 strips, 3½" x 42"; crosscut each strip into 11 squares, 3½" x 3½"

From the binding fabric, cut:
- 6 strips, 2½" x 42"

MAKING THE FLYING GEESE BLOCKS

One of the best things about sewing with friends is learning something new. I had always made my Flying Geese blocks using the traditional rotary-cut method, trimming both the background and "goose" fabrics ¼" from each seam. My friend Cindy Pope showed me how she leaves the rectangular goose fabric intact, scissor trimming only the background square. The blocks finish true to the size of the rectangle and lay beautifully flat. Try both methods and discover your own preference.

Assembling the Flying Geese with Clipped Wings

1. With right sides together, layer 1 light square over 1 dark rectangle, matching the corners. Draw a diagonal line from corner to corner on the wrong side of the square and sew on the line. Cut ¼" away from the line. Press the seam allowances open.

2. Repeat at the opposite corner.

3. Repeat to make a total of 64 Flying Geese blocks in this manner.

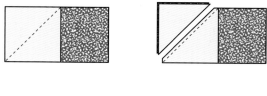

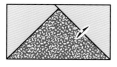

Make 64.

Assembling the Flying Geese without Clipped Wings

1. With right sides together, layer one light square over one dark rectangle. Draw a diagonal line from corner to corner on the wrong side of the square and sew on the line.

2. Cut only the light fabric ¼" from the line by folding the "goose" fabric corner back and trimming the light fabric with scissors. Trimming should be done neatly but need not be precise. Press the background triangle up over the dark fabric corner.

3. Repeat at the opposite corner.

4. Repeat to make a total of 64 Flying Geese blocks in this manner.

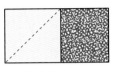 

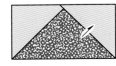

Make 64.

LAYING OUT THE QUILT

After you've made the Flying Geese blocks and cut the sashing triangles, lay out the entire quilt, referring to the layout diagram below. Each Flying Geese row has 16 blocks. Each sashing strip is composed of 7 large triangles and 1 small triangle at each end. Distribute the prints and colors until you are satisfied with the results.

Each Flying Geese row is made up of 16 blocks.

MAKING THE PIECED SASHING

1. Stitch 7 large triangles together into a row, off-setting the points by ¼". Press the seam allowances open. Repeat to make 5 sashing rows.

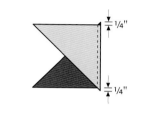

2. Sew one 6⅞" triangle to both ends of each row. Press the seam allowances open.

3. Trim the top and bottom edges of the sashing strip, removing the seam-allowance points.

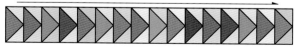

Make 5.

ASSEMBLING THE QUILT

1. Join the Flying Geese blocks into strips of 16, pressing the seam allowances away from the top of each "goose."

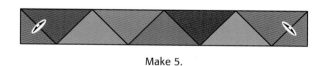

Make 4.

2. Pin the sashing strips to the Flying Geese strips, matching the centers, beginnings, and ends of the strips and matching seams where applicable. Stitch the rows together with the Flying Geese on top so that you can see the seam intersections more easily. Sewing directly through those intersections will help to maintain the points of the triangles.

FINISHING THE QUILT

1. Refer to "Quilting Basics" on page 89 as needed to finish your quilt. Prepare the quilt backing; then layer and baste the backing, batting, and quilt top together.

2. Quilt as desired.

3. Trim the excess batting and backing fabric, remove the basting, and bind your quilt. Use the six 2½"-wide strips for the binding.

4. Add a hanging sleeve if desired. Add a label or pocket to your quilt.

Sweet Sachets

Flying Geese blocks become swans when they're stuffed with lavender or other fragrant fillings. Add ribbons for hanging in a closet or tie a bundle with a beautiful ribbon to display on a dresser. These elegant sachets are too pretty to hide away in a drawer! Tuck them into a pretty china bowl from a yard sale or flea market, and you'll have a unique gift for a dear friend.

FINISHED SIZE: 3" x 6"

MATERIALS FOR EACH SACHET

2 rectangles of fabric, 3½" x 6½"

2 squares of fabric, 3½" x 3½"

About 1 cup of dried lavender, rosemary, or pine needles

Ribbon, tassels, or beads for embellishment

ASSEMBLING THE SACHETS

1. Make 1 Flying Geese block using a rectangle and 2 squares and following the instructions on page 81.

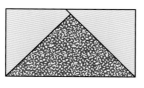

2. With right sides together, layer the remaining rectangle with the Flying Geese block. Stitch ¼" from the edges, leaving a 2½" to 3" opening.

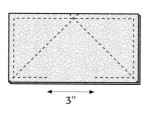

3. Clip the corners.

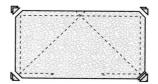

4. Turn the unit right side out. Fill with dried lavender, rosemary, or pine needles.

5. Hand stitch the opening closed. Add ribbons, tassels, or beads as desired.

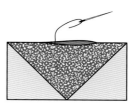

Finding a Location

Our grandparents' family cabin in Idaho is a wonderful place for my sister Julia and me to sew. The kitchen table becomes the sewing table, and the loft offers a great vantage point to study quilt blocks laid out on the living-room floor. Surrounded by family memories from four generations, it's a very special place to us. However, it's fairly remote: a ten-hour drive from home, two hours from the nearest quilt shop, and two miles from pavement and the nearest telephone. What's just perfect for "just us" wouldn't satisfy a crowd!

For a retreat, the larger a group of quilters is, the greater diversity of activities and sights will be needed to satisfy everyone's desires. Look for a town of a walkable size with a grocery store nearby and some great scenery. Nearby restaurants, bakeries, outlet malls, galleries, quaint shops—particularly quilt shops—are a bonus. You probably won't find it all in one town, but try to find what's most important to you, and chances are your friends will enjoy it, too.

If your retreat consists of four or fewer quilters, consider renting a hotel room or adjoining rooms. Weekend rates can be downright attractive, especially in a city where most hotels cater to business travelers. Ask about discounts or specials, and let the reservationist know that you're looking for a bargain. Clear the desk for your sewing machine and lay out blocks on the beds. Many hotel rooms are now equipped with irons and ironing boards, or they are available upon request. You have the added bonus of maid service, room service, and in-room movies. What a treat!

SLEEPING ACCOMMODATIONS

Check with your guests before you make the final decision on location, to find out how many beds will be needed. Someone may prefer a private room for health or personal reasons; most have probably weathered enough slumber parties and don't mind sharing rooms or even beds.

WORD OF MOUTH

If you're lucky enough to know someone with a lakeside cabin or beach house, you may already have a location. Be sure that you're clear about the owner's expectations regarding cleaning. Have all the guests sign a thank-you card to send from the retreat, and consider sending the owner a gift of thanks after your retreat.

RENTAL SERVICES

Renting a vacation house for your retreat is more cost-effective than you might think when you split the cost among ten guests. You may also have the benefits of the cleaning service that most property management services require, which means you won't be stressing out about not leaving your best friend's sister's mountain cabin in less-than-sparkling condition.

The Internet can be a wonderfully efficient way to scan an area for rental properties. Most property management services offer lists of amenities, including number of beds and bedrooms and photographs of several rooms so you can get a feel for the place. Look for a large common room, enough tables to set up sewing machines and cutting areas or room to bring in your own additional tables, and enough beds for everyone. Be sure to ask lots of questions:

- Is there ample parking?

- Can you move furniture to accommodate the sewing and cutting areas, or bring in extra folding tables?

- Are laundry facilities available, including iron and ironing board?

- What type of cleaning are you responsible for prior to departure?

- Is there a telephone for emergency contact, and what is the number?

- Are there any basic groceries available in the kitchen (oil, flour, salt, pepper, etc.)?

- Is the kitchen stocked with basic cookware and utensils, including coffeemaker?

If at all possible, make an advance visit before you make a final decision. When renting a property, you will be taking responsibility for the property by signing the agreements, so read them carefully. You will probably be required to post a security deposit to cover any damages, but it is usually refundable or applied to the rental charges.

WHAT YOU'LL NEED TO BRING

Tailor your packing list to reflect your location, the number of people, and what's available there. Some of the necessities and luxuries we've ended up packing include extra irons and ironing boards; rotary cutters, cutting boards, and rulers; folding tables; an extra coffee maker; extra sewing machines for emergencies; power strips and extension cords; and the most comfortable clothes we own!

Slumber Party Cookies

Our friend Maureen Reynolds gives everybody just what they want when she makes cookies for a crowd! Mix up a batch or two of this basic cookie recipe, and provide a smorgasbord of tasty mix-ins. Each friend transforms her own dough by adding just the right amount of her favorite cookie ingredients.

BASIC COOKIE RECIPE

2 cups (4 sticks) butter

1½ cups granulated sugar

1½ cups brown sugar

4 eggs

4 teaspoons vanilla

4½ cups all-purpose flour

2 teaspoons salt

2 teaspoons baking soda

Mix-ins (see list at right)

Cooking spray

1. Cream together butter and sugars.

2. Stir in eggs and vanilla.

3. Stir together flour, salt, and baking soda; then stir it into the dough.

4. For each participant, place ⅓ cup of dough into a small bowl (a coffee cup works great).

5. Everyone mixes in her favorite cookie treats! For each ⅓ cup of dough, stir in about 3 tablespoons of any combination of the additions listed in the box.

6. Drop by heaping tablespoonfuls onto a baking sheet sprayed with cooking spray. Bake at 375°F for 7 to 8 minutes for chewy cookies (the centers will remain soft) or 9 to 10 minutes for crisp cookies.

Favorite Mix-Ins
Chopped milk chocolate bars
Chopped bittersweet chocolate bars
Peanut butter chips
White chocolate chips
Toffee bits
Walnuts
Peanuts
Pecans
Macadamia nuts
Raisins
Dried cherries
Dates

Looking for a new favorite? Try these terrific combinations:

- Triple Threat: milk, dark, and white chocolates

- Granola Goodies: granola, peanuts, and raisins

- Tropical Dream: macadamias, white chocolate chips, and dates

- PBJ Crunch: peanuts, dried cherries, and peanut butter chips

- Mocha Latte: milk chocolate, 1 teaspoon instant coffee powder, and white chocolate chips

- White Christmas: dried cranberries, white chocolate chips, and walnuts

- Hula Chip: white chocolate chips and macadamia nuts

Each ⅓ cup of dough make about 3 cookies, for a total of approximately 72 cookies. However, this yield will depend on the number of mix-ins (more mix-ins = more cookies) and on how much dough you and your guests eat!

QUILTING BASICS

The most important thing about the basics of quilting is remembering that they are not the same for every person or even every project. For every tip that works for me, I learned different methods from at least three other accomplished quilters. What follows are descriptions of techniques I rely on, in hopes that you'll find a little gem that works for you.

YOUR MINDSET

No one quilts to add stress to their life! Every step, from choosing patterns and fabrics to stitching that last bit of binding, should be enjoyed. Let go, and don't worry about anyone else's version of right and wrong. But if your quilts are not satisfying to you, then you must step back and rewrite some of the rules that you quilt by, either consciously or unconsciously.

If you find that you are totally stuck in a creative ditch, give yourself permission to just play for a little while. Try out all your decorative stitches, sewing curvy rows just to enjoy the unusual textured shapes. Pick new colors of fabric that stretch your usual palette and use them to make a single block. This type of playing is not "just fooling around"; it's the muscle of your creative spirit. Exercise it and allow it to become strong and vibrant!

If there is something you really don't care to do, find a way around it! I don't really enjoy layering a quilt with safety pins, so when I do it I treat myself by popping a movie in the VCR or talking with a willing friend or one of my daughters. If you don't enjoy choosing fabrics, then invite along a friend whose taste you admire to offer some advice. There are always options!

The only rule I religiously follow is this: After two silly mistakes, I quit for awhile!

I enjoy teaching art literacy in my daughter's school. This is a program in which volunteers go into each classroom to show slides and discuss an artist's work, and then lead an art project at the grade level of each classroom. After around second grade, I often hear children say, "I'm not good at watercolors" or "I'm not good at drawing." This is heartbreaking, as they have already internalized the idea that one of their most important venues of self-expression is somehow flawed!

Many of the artists we now revere were once ridiculed for committing their contrarian personal visions to canvas: Rembrandt van Rijn, Vincent van Gogh, Paul Gauguin, and Henri Rousseau, to name just a few. They just stuck to it and created a personal style upon which we now place a high cultural and monetary value. You may not strive to hang your quilts in museums, but to refine your personal expressions and enjoy the process. It will show in your work and in the amount of satisfaction you find in each piece.

WASHING YOUR FABRICS

There are several considerations as you decide whether to prewash your fabrics: intended use, shrinkage, bleeding, and excessive fraying. I'll offer you my thoughts on this hotly debated quilting topic and allow you to be the ultimate decision maker in your own studio!

Treat the fabric prior to quilting just as you would the finished quilt. For example, a wall hanging may need only shaking out or vacuuming to remove dust, so prewashing is not necessary. On the other end of the spectrum, a baby quilt will be washed repeatedly, so wash the fabrics before quilting just as you would expect to wash the quilt. If you don't wash the fabrics first, but do wash the finished quilt, be prepared for some puckering. Usually it's not drastic and may even serve to create a more antique look.

If you do choose to prewash, you may be able to cut down on fraying in one of several ways. Clip at an angle each of the four corners of the yardage. Trim the edge with pinking shears or a rotary pinking blade. Add a basting stitch to the cut edge of each piece of yardage. However, the yardage requirements in this book and those of most patterns take the effects of fraying into account.

Last but not least, as you prepare to make a group quilt, you must ask all the contributors to treat the fabric that they use in the same way.

MAKING ENDS MEET

All of the quilts in this book are designed with a group of contributing quilters in mind. Because each quilter has a slightly different ¼" seam allowance, measures with different rulers in different ways, and comes at the project with differing skill levels, you may need to entice the blocks to fit together well! Try the following techniques to fine-tune points and seams so you end up with a quilt that you and the rest of the group will be proud of.

Squaring Up

Squaring up is the simplest method of ensuring that blocks from more than one quilter will fit together neatly. Start by measuring a variety of blocks; are they all at least as large as the pattern instructions call for? If so, just trim the edges as necessary to bring them all to the same size as well as to square them up.

If some of the blocks are larger and some are significantly smaller, you may make a judgment call to square the larger blocks to a slightly smaller size. Be aware that doing so may alter the design of the finished quilt! You may opt to separate the blocks by size and use the "orphan" blocks to assemble other projects: table runners, pillow tops, or baby quilts.

Short Seaming

If, after squaring up the blocks, they still differ in size by ⅛" or less, you can still wind up with a great, flat quilt by paying close attention to the short blocks as you assemble the top. Identify all of the short blocks; they may all be made from the same fabrics, or if not, use colored pins as markers.

As you sew the blocks into rows, pay special attention to these short blocks, and position them carefully as you join them to the other blocks. The cut edge of the short block won't meet the edge of the other block. On the back of the quilt, the seam allowance for these short blocks will be smaller but should be at least ⅛".

Easing-In Techniques

Easing in means making gentle and generous use of your steam iron and pins as you assemble the blocks. Steam or water spray will help the cotton fibers in your pieced top to expand or contract slightly to achieve matched corners and points. Your results will vary depending on the individual fabrics used; easing in can make a really positive difference in your finished quilt. In general terms, easing in can help in matching seams if you're dealing with a difference of up to ¼" in a 4" to 6" block, depending on the fabrics involved.

To fit a piece that is slightly too small, pin one end's seam allowance into its correct position. Spray the piece lightly with water and pull the piece very gently to expand it. Pin the other end of the piece in its correct position and stretch it gently to fit. Apply the iron gently, for a few seconds at a time, until the fabric is thoroughly dry. Repeat as necessary; then stitch.

To fit a piece that is slightly too large, pin both seam allowances into their correct positions. Distribute the excess fabric in half and pin the correct middle of the piece into place. Repeat this "halving" of the excess until you have pins as close as every ¼". Spray the piece lightly with water, and press the iron gently to the edges of the piece to allow the heat to contract the cotton fibers. Continue to apply the iron gently until the fabric is thoroughly dry; then stitch.

Be warned that a quilt pieced with many large ease-ins may not lie perfectly flat in the end. If the blocks vary widely, you may want to consider squaring them to a smaller size.

Pinning

Pins are a quilter's basic because they help keep fabrics from pulling out of alignment as you sew. Insert pins at an angle to hold the seam allowances in place as you join rows, whether your seams are pressed open or to one side. If you pin your seam allowances as shown below, they'll meet neatly and lie flat, reducing bulk and making quilting easier.

Seam allowances pressed to one side. Seam allowances pressed open.

Spray Sizing

Another lifesaver in our studio is spray sizing. Lighter than starch, it is especially helpful if you are working with fabrics of different textures or with bias edges. A light spray of sizing during ironing gives drapey fabrics with a soft hand a bit of a "backbone" and will help prevent slipping or

stretching against other, stiffer fabrics. Flannels are another good candidate for sizing, particularly if you are using a variety of different flannels. Because flannels are produced by many manufacturers, there is a wide variance in the weight and finish that can cause the fabric to stretch while it is sewn.

Pressing and Ironing

Just being aware of the differences between pressing and ironing can make a world of difference in your quilting.

When pressing, your iron is primarily moving up and down, which keeps the fabric stable. Pressing is useful for setting seams prior to opening them, or putting seam allowances in their place.

Ironing is primarily moving the iron back and forth, encouraging the fabric to move as well. Ironing is useful when you're urging block edges to meet prior to seaming, or to remove wrinkles.

For example, using the tip and edge of your iron to push open a half-square triangle can result in a very crooked seam if you use an ironing motion, whereas a less "pushy" pressing motion will keep it as straight as when it was sewn. Conversely, ironing takes advantage of the stretchy properties of cotton, as when you're easing a short or skewed block into place. Of course, sometimes you'll combine the motions, but being aware of their effects will help to improve your results.

ADDING BORDERS

If your quilt has more than one border, apply this method to each one for a flat, square finish.

1. Measure the quilt top vertically, down the middle, to find the measurement for the side borders. If necessary, piece the border strips together for length and trim them to this measurement. Stitch these borders to the pieced quilt top on both sides, using easing-in techniques as necessary.

2. Measure the quilt top from side to side to find the measurement for the top and bottom borders. If necessary, piece the border strips for length, and trim to this measurement. Stitch

these borders to the pieced quilt top on the top and the bottom, using easing-in techniques, as necessary.

3. In general, press border seams away from the center of the quilt and toward the outer border.

PREPARING THE BACKING

Backing fabric should generally be 3" to 5" larger than the quilt top on all sides. The amount of extra backing fabric can be reduced proportionately for smaller projects. Adjust the yardage requirements and seaming, as necessary, if you are matching a directional print on the back.

A creatively pieced backing is a great way to use up leftover yardage and blocks from the quilt. Stitch them together in any fashion to create all or part of the backing. Adjust the listed yardage accordingly.

Unless otherwise specified, follow this method to prepare backing for any of the quilts in this book, using the specified yardage:

1. Cut the backing fabric in half, perpendicular to the selvage.

2. Place the two pieces right sides together.

3. Using a rotary cutter and ruler, cut off the selvage edges on one side.

4. Seam the trimmed side with a ½" seam allowance.

5. Press the seams open.

LAYERING THE PROJECT

I use the services of a professional quilter with a long-arm quilting machine for many of the quilt tops that I make, so I don't do the layering myself. When I do layer a quilt, I typically tape the backing to the floor in my den, smooth the batting over it, and safety pin it like crazy.

Spray basting works well for any project that can be quilted in one sitting, such as quilted pillow tops or table runners. Once again, choose your favorite method, or try something new and you can then add it to your own quilting repertoire.

QUILTING

There are many options for quilting designs, and each one will add something distinctive and special to your projects. A wonderful resource for quilting inspiration is *Quilting Makes the Quilt* by Lee Cleland, who has supplemented a wealth of information on design, materials, marking, and methods with inspirational examples of the depth and vivacity that quilting provides to a project.

A professional quilter, using a long-arm quilting machine, quilted all of the larger quilts in this book. If you choose this option, talk with other quilters or local quilt shops to get references. The quilting design, thread color, delivery date, and price range should always be clearly discussed and even written down when you give your project to a professional quilter.

Most of the small projects were quilted using a regular home sewing machine with an attached walking foot. Several of the projects were quilted using decorative stitches. No matter how you choose to quilt your project, always try out your design on a small scrap "quilt" as identical as possible to your finished piece. In doing so, you can troubleshoot the curves or corners of the quilting design, stitch width or length, needle position, thread colors and weight, machine tension, and more to prevent the heartbreak of having to rip quilting out of an otherwise exciting project.

ADDING THE BINDING

If you have not quilted all the way to the edge of the quilt top, attach a walking foot and baste the quilt top slightly less than ¼" from the edge using a spaced-out zigzag or straight stitch. This will reduce the possibility of the layers bunching up unevenly as you attach the binding. Choose the type of binding that's best for your project.

Pieced Binding

A creatively pieced binding will add one more playful element to a lighthearted quilt. To make a pieced binding, use the fabrics left over from the construction of the quilt top, cutting 2½"-wide strips of varying lengths from about 8" to 15". Cut enough strips to provide the length needed to bind the quilt and join them following the basic binding method described below.

Traditional Binding

For a traditional binding, cut 2½"-wide strips.

Binding for a Small Project

For a small project such as a table runner, try using a 2"-wide strip. The finished binding will be narrower and more in scale with the project.

Bias Binding

By cutting your binding strips at a 45-degree angle to the selvage, you will be able to create bias binding that will lie smoothly around the curved edges of your project.

Basic Binding Method

1. With right sides together, join the strips by overlapping the ends at right angles.

2. Draw a line diagonally from corner to corner and stitch on the line. Trim the corners ¼" from the seam.

3. Press the seams open.

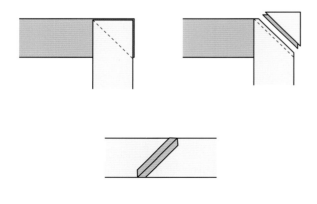

4. Trim the beginning end of the binding at a 45-degree angle; turn the angled edge under ¼" and press.

5. Fold the length of the binding strip in half and press.

Fold line

6. Beginning several inches from a corner, and keeping raw edges even, sew the binding to the front of the quilt using a ¼" seam allowance.

7. Stop sewing ¼" from the approaching corner and backstitch. Remove the quilt from the sewing machine.

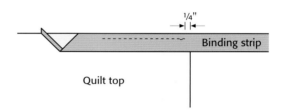

¼"

Binding strip

Quilt top

8. Fold the binding up to create a 45-degree angle, and then back down to align the raw edges of the quilt and the binding. Beginning at the edge, resume sewing the binding to the quilt. Repeat for the remaining corners.

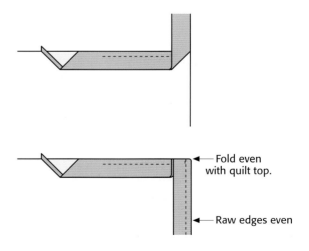

Fold even with quilt top.

Raw edges even

9. Fold the end piece of the binding into the starting end, overlapping by 2" to 3". Pin the overlap into place and complete the seam.

10. Turn the folded edge of the binding to the back of the quilt, forming miters at the corners. Blindstitch in place, being sure to cover the seam.

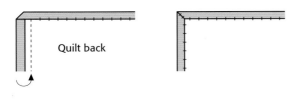

Quilt back

ADDING A LABEL

A label adds a true finishing touch to a quilt as well as the opportunity for giving credit to the talented individuals involved in its creation. Use any medium that suits you: embroidery, permanent fabric pens, appliqué, or a combination of methods. At the very least, be sure to record names and dates. Dress it up by adding freehand or traced designs, a verse or poem, signatures, and if you can bear to give your beautiful quilt away, the name of the lucky person who will receive it. Hem the label edges and blindstitch the label to the back of the quilt.

ADDING A POCKET

A pocket is a delightful way to keep treasured mementos with the quilt. What to put inside? For a gift quilt, tuck in a hemmed piece of cotton with a poem or sentiment written on it, charms, small heirlooms, or lucky coins. On an antique quilt, a letter-size pocket can hold information about the history of the quilt or its maker. For a child's quilt, add one or more pockets to hold a small flashlight, tiny toys, or a bedtime prayer or verse.

After you've decided what to tuck in, cut two pieces of fabric, one for the pocket and one for the flap. Cut them at least ½" larger than the size of the object, taking the bulk of the enclosed object into account. Fold over each edge ¼", press, and hem stitch ⅛" from the edge on all sides. Pin the pieces to the quilted quilt, positioning the pocket and flap to accommodate the enclosure. Blindstitch by hand to the back of the quilt. Add a button, snap, ribbon tie, or Velcro closure if desired.

BIBLIOGRAPHY

Cleland, Lee. *Quilting Makes the Quilt.* Bothell, Wash.: Martingale & Company, 1994.

Hopkins, Judy. *Around the Block with Judy Hopkins.* Bothell, Wash.: Martingale & Company, 1994.

McClun, Diana and Nownes, Laura. *Quilts! Quilts!! Quilts!!!: The Complete Guide to Quiltmaking.* Lincolnwood, Ill.: The Quilt Digest Press, 1997.

ABOUT THE AUTHOR

Anne Moscicki's childhood love of art and drawing grew into an award-winning career in design and art direction. When her sister Julia taught her to quilt with rotary-cutting techniques seven years ago, she joyfully redis-covered the sense of craft that she had loved early in her profession. Combining her love of quilting and her design background resulted in the creation of Touchwood Quilt Design with partner Linda Wyckoff. She lives in Oregon with her husband, two daughters, and a very spoiled West Highland terrier.

Photo by David Lutz